Body Language

Ultimate Guide To Learn The Secrets Non-verbal Body Cues And Mastering Social Skills

(Master Speed Reading People Through Body Language Analysis And Psychology Tricks)

Rob C Beckham

Published By **Tyson Maxwell**

Rob C Beckham

Body Language: Ultimate Guide To Learn The Secrets Non-verbal Body Cues And Mastering Social Skills (Master Speed Reading People Through Body Language Analysis And Psychology Tricks)

ISBN   978-1-77485-915-5

No part of this guidebook shall be reproduced in any form without permission in writing from the publisher except in the case of brief quotations embodied in critical articles or reviews.

Legal & Disclaimer

Table of Contents

Chapter 1: What Is Body Language & Business Communications?

Communication is key to business connections.

Communication is crucial, regardless of whether it's the carefully planned advertising you use to attract your intended interest group, or the discussions that you have to foster organization development with partners.

While both written and verbal communication have their place within the corporate world, non-verbal communication is just as important. Non-verbal communication can be as simple as the way that you present yourself to others in a group or how well you resolve to eye-to eye connection. These things can either harm or help the message you're trying to send.

The foundation for business communication that is non-verbal allows people to talk with one another at a deeper level. You can transmit the most important information from your appearance to your body movements.

What is Body Language?

The implicit component of communication, which we use to communicate our emotions and feelings, is body language. You can see our signals through outward appearances and

posture.

When we "read" these signs, it is possible to use it for our benefit. It can assist us in understanding what someone is trying tell us and improve our awareness of their responses.

It is also possible to use it for non-verbal communication improvement, so we are more open, receptive and engaging.

Sometimes our actions can be more powerful than our words.

In case you're wondering why body language is essential in business communications you need to first understand the way body language adds value to any discussion.

To make a nuanced communication, body language can be described as a strengthening idea. There are many possibilities for non-verbal communication in body language. Non-verbal communication is, for instance:

* A substitute: Sometimes body language can be used in place of verbal communication. In the case of a partner who won't stop talking, for instance, you cannot simply tell them to stop talking. You have the option to look at your watch and/or venture back to show them that you are going.

* Regulatory. Customers or workers can use body language to guide a discussion. A gathering meeting might have different non-verbal prompts that indicate when one

person can start talking and the other must end.

* A complementing speech approach: Sometimes body language in business can help to enhance your verbal communication. You may, for example, point at a subject that you are discussing.

* Repetitive. In business communications, body language can be used to rehash and draw attention to a thought. To remind workers to bring the sign-in sheets to work, you can either point at it or lift the sheet.

Body language is crucial in business communications. Your body language will have a significant impact on how your customers and representatives perceive you. According to analysts and researchers, body language and other non-verbal communication in the business sector are often much more extravagant than unneeded words. Chances are that you have been hurt or frustrated by someone in the past.

The ability to communicate non-verbally with others can be a key factor in the success of a business. Partners use non-verbal communication to push customers to buy. Activities can be driven more effectively by the things you say than what you say.

Be aware of how you communicate with others in your business.

A few people are unable to stand someone who stalls slowly as they walk. In certainty, they won't hire an individual who moves that way because it educates a lot about them. What are your non-verbal communications saying about you

Chapter 2: How Is The World Viewing You

In my senior year of college, I had an acquaintance who struggled to communicate with large groups of people and especially girls. He was the one guy I knew who didn't have a date at the movies or at the pool parties. He came alone, stayed by himself, and left. The man was brilliant and charming once he got to know you, but the world wasn't seeing that side of his personality, which is why nobody ever gave him a chance.

This was the first time he applied for a internship at a company where he truly wanted to work. He made it all the the way to the interview. He is smart and extremely hardworking, so it was an easy decision for me. I felt confident that he was far more qualified than any other interviewees. However, the interviewer refrained from believing it. I asked him why he didn't believe they would accept his application. He said that they loved everything I had submitted. It was the last interview that let me down. I was dumbfounded as the lady kept asking me question after question. She was still puzzled that I had filled out the application, given my personal experience. Even though I wanted so much to share, I couldn't. It was as if something was holding my back."

Poor boy struggled with exactly what I want us all to tackle in this chapter. He was right. He was held back by some thing. I don't want you to feel that anguish.

Do You See What You Are Looking At When You Look in The Mirror?

We often struggle to express our self confidently because of low self-esteem. Most people don't feel enough love for themselves. I don't mean a superficial type of love. I mean unconditional, true love. To love yourself, one must understand themselves.

I know many guys who have difficulty maintaining loving, healthy relationships.

Whatever excuses you might make, the fact remains, that you will never attract and keep the affection of another man if you don't know how you love yourself. Without a good relationship with yourself, it's impossible to know how you love yourself. Have you ever been on a first date with yourself just to get to know yourself better? If that sounds unusual, you can start by taking small steps.

Mirror work is a method that helps you see yourself as you really are. It was the first step in my journey to changing my life. It was important to understand the world's perceptions of me in order to make it more my own. I started to spend a lot of my time alone. In my early years I used the mirror to examine myself and see who I was. The mirror was my first tool to see who I really was. It revealed that he was hidden under layers of false beliefs, habits, unchecked emotions, and layers of my own thoughts that projected what I didn't want.

My body language from the past has made me look desperate, closed-up and sometimes tense. I am naturally more introverted but in my past I was quite quiet and rarely made eye-contact. I had a neutral expression during conversations with people. Recording myself in conversations with friends revealed that I often had my arms and legs crossed. Also, my voice was weak and lacking confidence. After spending several weeks in my apartment, I became more comfortable looking into the mirror and started to recognize areas that required improvement.

We tend to think that looking in the Mirror or self-care is synonymous with narcissism. However, I can tell you that self-care, and taking time to see yourself in the mirror, are profound and almost spiritual. The mirror can be used to learn more about yourself. It can help you improve self-compassion and self-love. Once you have learned to be compassionate, it will be easy to do the same for others. It helps you be more conscious of your body movements, facial expressions, and other aspects. Spend seven days in front of a mirror, or recording yourself whenever possible, even when it comes to mundane tasks like eating, chilling, or talking to someone. You will learn a lot about your own behavior and how it affects others. Do not be surprised if you find out that sometimes what you think and actually see are often in conflict. Do not want to spend too much time recording yourself. Instead, get a small mirror that you can keep handy and place it where you see it frequently. It's an excellent way to learn about yourself and your body language. Spending time with your mirror in front can help you discover hidden beliefs and emotions that may be holding you back.

Develop Your Body Language

After you spend time with you and start to notice your body language, then you are able to transform it into what you want. These are some suggestions to improve your body communication.

* Sit straight. While this is as basic as it gets many of us don't realize how important our posture is. Pay attention to how many people are slumping when you go out in public, such as a coffee shop or restaurant. You can look more confident if you don't slouch. Instead, I encourage you to sit straight with a straight back and a relaxed spine.

Smiling more will help you relax and soften your gaze. If you, like me, are aware that your facial expressions may need some improvement, one of my first recommendations is to practice laughter and gaze intently in the face of the person in front. You can start this by using the mirror. Start smiling and see how it changes your face. If you feel confident with your smile, then share it with others in a conversation.

* Try to minimize distracting movements that might make you look anxious or uncomfortable.

* Keep eye contact comfortable and natural. I don't want you looking weird due to your

intense stare. However, I do recommend you make as much eye contact possible. This may seem difficult initially because you might not be used seeing people in the eye. Practice with your mirror. Eye contact is essential. You will notice how your eyes adjust as you say different things to your self, such as "thanks" or "I'm so proud of you", and you will feel the natural progression towards restoring your eye contact. You can think of it as a dance among lovers. Sometimes you can pull in the person using your eyes. If that happens, you let them go and look at something for a pause. This will become easier with time.

It will make you more confident by training your arms and hands to move with more control. Instead of fidgeting or throwing your hands around while walking, your hands can be used to improve your posture. Telling a story to someone is a great way to use your hands. If the listener can understand your body language, they will too.

* Mirror the other person. After taking some time to reflect, you can begin to see the best in yourself. It's best to mirror others naturally. Mirroring can be a powerful way to build a bond with someone if it is done well. A good example of mirroring someone is when they lean forward and wait a few seconds before naturally leaning forward. If the person nods and continues, mirror them. Timing is everything. You don't want your immediate reaction to be copied.

What if You Have an RBF

Natural features that some people have are known as bitchy resting faces (RBF) and resting bitch. It's a phenomena that has caused a lot of debate and discussion. Science researchers have shown that RBF is real, and have tried to explain why it occurs. But I know for certain that most people would prefer to have rid of it. Abbe Macbeth, a behavioral researcher from Noldus Information Technology in international research and development decided to investigate. Noldus's

FaceReader (a complex tool engineered) was used by the pair to identify certain expressions based upon a collection of more than 10,000 images. Their software is capable of viewing faces with a live cam, a photo, and / or video clips. It then starts mapping out five-hundred points on the human facial features. Then it can analyse and assign expressions based upon the eight most basic emotions. These emotions include sadness and happiness, anger as well fear, surprise, contempt and disgust. Rogers and Macbeth started the experiment by creating a series genuinely expressionless facial images using FaceReader. The benchmark of a face expressing little to no emotion is about 3%. These blank faces showed 3% emotion, and 97% was neutral. The software celebrity faces were then fed, and the emotion levels jumped from three percent to six percent. Macbeth explained that the significant drop in percentage resulted from 'contempt. The experiment showed them that RBF wasn't a purely female phenomenon. While it's possible for men to experience it as well, at the moment it's more prevalent in women.

Celebrities such as Victoria Beckham, Kirsten Stuart, and even Kanye West have been known for their RBFs. Some people enjoy it and wear it all the time, while others, such as Jenny, would be happy to give it up.

Jenny has had bouts of depression since she was a teenager. Jenny and I share a common childhood. We went to the same schools, churches, and other activities. From as far back as my memory can remember. She has always said that people tend to say something about her facial appearance that is unapproachable. She feels like people judge and criticize her because they feel she is judging others. Because of this, it has been very difficult for her to make friends. Even when I take her to a party with my friend, she won't move and will just wait for people to come. At the end, she will say something like, "There's no way I can fix it." It's not that I can get a different face or something. It's not clear whether or not it is a learned defense mechanism. RBF people can feel disapproval, but we don't have the right to make a blanket statement because every person is different. You can make your life easier, and you will be able to get along better with people, by softening your RBF. Here's how you can improve your RBF.

* Try pranayama toga or om singing. This will help you grow spiritually, emotionally and physically. It can also be used to exercise the muscles needed to reduce RBF.

Regularly work out your throat and head. If you love musical instruments, this is the time to get started.

* Pay attention and pay close attention to the way you move your eyes. You might notice they appear more sad, so when you look at someone, try looking upwards.

* If you are a women, apply makeup. Correctly applying makeup to your eyes can

transform downcast eyes in to more open, brighter eyes.

* Smile while engaging your cheekbones. You will appear more alert and awake if your cheekbones are engaged in a deliberate manner.

* Learn to smile more. We have all been in environments that discourage smiling and encourage joy. Perhaps you were raised by an angry or abusive parent. You may experience permanent changes to your facial expressions. It would be very unnatural to smile in such situations. You will need practice, patience, practice, and a mirror in order to learn how to smile more often. You can soften your expressions and raise your cheeks if you don't manage to smile.

* Practice forgiveness. Recognize that your RBF may be hiding contempt. It's not enough to fake smile and use makeup. You must address your internal problems. Forgiveness is key. It is possible to choose to end that burden. Unresolved bitterness or anger,

remorseful, regret, or other forms of oppression can be a burden. Do yourself a favor. See how much lighter and happier your body will feel.

Don't let anything stop you.

I was once told a story about a man whose life was upended by the closing of the biggest deal. During negotiations, he got a call from an emergency letting him understand that his wife had just given birth to their first child and was being rushed by the hospital. They had been trying to get a child for years. This was a significant moment for him. He was overwhelmed by emotions when he got the call. He was just an hour from the hospital, still in the middle a deal which depended on his health. What did he do to calm down? He took a deep, slow breath, calmed down, put on his poker face and returned to the conference room, where he was able to focus on the sale. It was impossible to find out the man's thoughts and feelings in that meeting. However, the deal secured him the promotion of VP of sales. Life is unpredictable and throws many curveballs at us, both positive and negative. How do we handle that?

For most people, any time they are confronted with news or a situation that feels uncontrollable leads to an immediate outburst. Everything is affected. Focus, calmness and concentration are all lost. If it is something negative, anger and resentment, yelling, or outrage can be expressed. It might be excitement, joy, nervousness or all of the above. but it would still throw him off his game.

Not only must we manage our emotions, but it is also our job to control our natural impulses and reactions when faced with unanticipated news. I don't mean the large reactions that can be seen from a distance. Also, subtle micro-expressions are often transmitted from the body.

This term "pokerface" might be something you've heard in a variety of settings. It's not only relevant in Las Vegas. Many business leaders are skilled at making poker faces. It is one of many best-kept secrets that allows successful leaders to hide and control their emotions. Don't fall for it. While this skill is not something you'll naturally develop, with practice anyone can improve their ability to remain cool and calm when under pressure.

You must not crack under pressure.

Did you notice how cool and calm Dominic Toretto (the main character in Fast and Furious), is even when everything seems to go to hell? It's one reason his fans love him. Being able to maintain that level of control makes you both a powerful driver and a powerful person. You can be a leader, no matter what your circumstances. Don't let anyone tell you anything, even if it is disappointing or nerve-wracking. Instead, you can try these techniques.

Relax your facial muscles. A more relaxed face means it is easier for someone else to discern what you are thinking.

* Pause for 60 seconds. Allow yourself to take a few moments for yourself. Then, check-in. Keep silent for sixty seconds, regardless of how strongly you want something to happen. If you're calling, please say "Thank you" and hang up. If it is in person, apologize and say thank you. This is important to allow you time to do the next steps.

* Breathe. Take a deep breath. Slowly exhale. You will feel your heartbeat slow down as you continue to deep breathe. Many leaders publicly stated that deep breathing for at least a minute helps them to focus and make sense of situations.

* Assess your body language and facial expressions. Take note of your posture. Are you standing tall and confident or are you slumping? Are your shoulders tight? Adjust them. Are your eyes blinking far too much? Is your jaw locked? Are your cheeks becoming hot? Be aware of what's going on around you and accept the change for a while. Then, change it to be what you want.

Chapter 3: The Brain And Body Language Perception

When you hear the words "boss," what comes to mind is an authoritative, powerful, and straightforward man/woman who, regardless of how long you have worked with them, is still intimidating. Many people still struggle to get along with their boss, even though they have been working with them for many years. You don't have to be a difficult person to communicate with - you just need confidence and sometimes some wit.

Some employees fear their boss's presence and others are afraid to approach him. It is important to have a sense of certainty. Being able to discern your boss' mood, and to know what he or she is feeling, will allow you to approach your boss with confidence. You can also create a positive impression for yourself. Knowing your boss is a powerful tool. If you can recognize key body language indicators and understand what they are saying, you will be a step ahead!

The Handshake

Pay attention to the gestures and postures of your boss. Employers tend to hold their hands down when giving a handshake. If they do this, you will accept it with your face up. You are eventually submissive to the boss and he is superior to yourself. It's very difficult to reverse this. This is because superior people compete for dominance, superiority and their egos. If they were submissive, it would damage their egos. What are you going to do? What are you going to do to show the boss you are not just a normal, submissive employee. Next time, you can do a double-grip: take the handshake and accept it submissively, but firmly. Then use your other hand for handicapping his hand. You're giving him the impression you're not a sheep.

Eye focus

Your eyes are a powerful indicator of a person's character. Also, the eyes can be used to communicate body language. It is easy to see how a person feels by the way they look. This can also be a way to see how your boss is relating to you. If you are trying to make friends with your boss but you notice his eyes glued to his wristwatch or his papers, you should reconsider your strategy. This is a sign that your boss doesn't care about your presence. You might also notice your boss looking at other things while you chat with him. To tell if a conversation goes well, you have to notice the other party looking at your face with attentive eyes. This is a sign of interest and a sign that you are having a good conversation.

Critical Evaluation and Touch-To-Face Gestures

The hand-toface gesture signals that you are ready for a thorough evaluation. This position involves one finger supporting the thumb and the index finger pointed up at the cheek.

Another sign that someone is having a critical review is when their arms and legs are tightly crossed. This signals that they are making a negative and defensive non-verbal statement. This is a sign that your boss is having a critical discussion about your presentation. If your boss does this, it is best to either change your idea or politely dismiss your boss.

Mirroring

A lot of people fear their boss for making them feel inferior. Mirror your boss's actions but not in a disrespectful or mocking way. Mirroring is a way to show how close your relationship with someone. Two friends who are very close may mimic each others' postures involuntarily (clapping, smiling, etc.). Mirroring someone isn't a prerequisite. Faking it while talking to a friend can make your relationship more successful. To be close to your boss, emulate his or her actions. Be strong, speak up, and believe in yourself.

Superiority

It's a horrible feeling to walk into your boss' office and begin talking about a meeting. Then suddenly, your boss holds onto your hands and places them behind your head. This gesture shows superiority. Your boss may be boasting about what he is really trying to convey. This gesture often means, "Ha!" I'm much more powerful than yours" or, even, "Yes! Someday maybe when I become smarter than you. . You will be annoyed by the act of it all, even if they are not directly said. Mirror this gesture the next time you see it. Your boss will be able to tell that something is wrong and will immediately take steps to change his or her mind. Their next gesture would be to cross their arms - it suggests inner defense.

Be sure to identify group clusters in body language before you attempt to decipher it. Here are some scenarios you might have experienced when communicating with your boss.

John is a hardworking and dedicated businessman. He was with his company for five year. He was happy to stay at his company for five years, but he wanted to rise in the ranks so he asked for a raise. First thing John saw was his boss, seated in his high-back and comfortable chair. John approached him with great fear and then sat down on a nearby chair. He doesn't know how to respond. He crossed his arms and crossed his legs. Then he tap anxiously on the folder in front of him, an obvious sign he is nervous and unprepared. John continued to speak in a stuttering tone, avoiding the gaze of his boss. The room was filled up with dead air until the boss stopped. He then clasped both his hands and put them behind him. The boss looked at John and inquired if John was going in to request a raise. John's eyes lit as the boss revealed his true intent. He felt ashamed, as he thought he might fail to meet the requirements. His confidence is eventually destroyed by this attitude. John was not asked to give his company information and accomplishments. Instead, he handed the boss a folder and sat still while he went through them. He was then given back his files by the boss. He touched his nose and then rubbed them. After that, he said "John, I will consider it." Finally, he gave John his handshake, signaling the close of the discussion.

What would have been the outcome if the body language had been acknowledged? And if the approach was different? This is an alternative scene:

John is a hardworking and dedicated businessman. He was with his company for five year. He wanted to rise in the ranks and so he asked for a raise from his boss. First thing he noticed was his boss sitting in his high and comfortable chair. With a smile on face, he walked to his boss's chair, complimenting his tie and engaging in a brief conversation. After having a great time, John got the attention and approval of his boss. John explained his business, and asked for an increase. The boss demanded information about his company's achievements and profile. John provided the documents. After scanning the files the boss asked John some questions. John answered the questions with confidence and followed his boss' gestures. The boss was now comfortable with the fellow and stood to offer him a handshake. John agreed to the handshake and then left the office.

What were the simple gestures made by the body? Why didn't they give us a different result?

Here's another scenario:

Linda is a recent employee. She strives for a strong relationship with everyone in her workplace. One day, during lunch, Linda met her boss in the hallway of the canteen. This gave her the opportunity to meet the boss in the canteen hallway. She welcomed him and began a conversation. Linda noticed her boss constantly checking his watch while they were communicating. She was aware of what this meant, but she still continued to communicate. Linda spoke about a lot more than she was interested in, which made matters worse. He replied by looking at anywhere but Linda, indicating boredom and disinterest. John, Linda's coworker, approached John. He immediately apologized and took advantage of the opportunity.

This alternate scene is:

Linda is a recent employee. She strives for a strong relationship with everyone in her workplace. She had lunch with her boss and met him in the hallway of the canteen. At this moment, she approached the boss and began to have a conversation. Linda noticed that her boss kept looking at the watch of her boss throughout their conversation. She saw what this meant. As soon as she realized it, she changed the subject to discuss something that was of interest to them both. Linda mirrors her boss and the conversation went well. Linda's boss was then comfortable and started to mirror Linda. John, John's coworker approached her boss and he politely declined to talk.

Remember that your boss likes to be a boss, superior, and competitive. These traits are what create his or her image. Your boss will appreciate you being both a leader but also a follower. If you submit too much, your boss may believe that you're not competent and not worthy of a promotion. You could be fired if you try to lead too much. Can you really say, "Sir. This is a way for me to prove my worth but not to take your job?"? It is best to communicate this message using body language. When you understand what your boss means verbally and not-verbally, it will make it easier to create a more relaxed and friendly atmosphere when you speak with them.

Chapter 4: Sweaty Hands Are A Huge Turnoff

Take a moment to appreciate the beauty of your surroundings. Consider the symmetry of your table. Admire the intricate craftsmanship of the flower vase or painting in this room. If you have the chance, go to your local museum or art gallery and take in all of the creativity that went into creating those masterpieces. This moment is when you can appreciate the creativity that brought those objects to life.

Our hands are unique. We communicate with the outside world using our hands. Our hands are expressive. Our hands are expressive. We can tell a story with our hands or share our innermost thoughts. It is important to learn how to use hand gestures to communicate nonverbal behaviors. Our brain directs our hands both consciously, and unconsciously.

How hand movements can boost your credibility and persuasiveness

Your hands can be the most effective way to express your feelings to the outside world. People tend to be more focused on the movements of their hands and fingers than they are on the rest. Why? It comes down to evolution again. As humans evolved, and moved into a more upright position, our hands became expressive, more skilled, and more dangerous.

Because of this, we tend not to pay attention to hand movements in order to understand what people are saying or if they have bad intentions. People perceive those who are expressive in their hand movements as convincing and trustworthy.

Keep an eye out for those who cover their tracks!

Experience has shown me that people are often hiding things from others when they cover their hands. If you hide your hands, those who understand the role of hand movements when reading nonverbal signs will likely view you suspiciously. If the hands are not visible, it can distract from the truth and quality of the information being transmitted.

The Appearance Of the Hand Speaks Volumes

It is easy to see the hands of a person and assess their work. People who spend all day typing on a computer will notice a more delicate, slender appearance to their hands. Contrarily, a laborer's hands will appear rough and calloused.

Calluses can form on the fingers of a guitarist or pianist. Athletes have more scarring than average people.

People should also consider how people care for their hands when they interact with them. People who have neatly manicured long nails are viewed as people who value social conventions. Nail biting is often seen to be a sign insecurity or nervousness.

Sweaty hands are a huge turnoff

Sweaty hands make it difficult to shake hands. If your hands become sweaty, your handshake can be clammy or weak. If your hands are easily moistened, it is a good idea to dry them. Not only is it the result of hot or tropical weather, but your hands can also become dry and sweaty if you are stressed out or anxious.

Be aware that sweaty hands are not a sign of deceit.

Analyze People by Their Handshakes

Did you ever feel your hand be crushed when you held hands with someone else? Perhaps you have ever been put off by a weak handshake. People don't realize that their first touch with another person is the most important point of contact.

The handshake is the most important moment in a relationship. You'll get a sense of the person that you are dealing.

Some people see a simple handshake and turn it into an opportunity for dominance. This can be annoying because it is an intentional attempt to subdue one party.

Others go further, using the "politicians' handshake," where the left side of the hand is covered by the right. These types handshakes tend not to make a good first impression but alienate.

Consider Cultural Differences

Cultural differences can be a significant factor in analyzing people. Two men holding hands for a long time in the Middle East is considered an indication of respect. In Western cultures, you are more likely to get stares from people who try to do this.

It is important that you understand the culture, norms and traditions of any destination you intend to visit. If someone from the Middle East and other parts Asia wishes to hold your hand, they should! It's not unusual for your Russian male host to kiss you on the cheek. You don't have to rebuke these gestures. It warms people up and makes it easier to analyze.

Tired, or Tensed

We've seen how effective facial expressions can make nonverbal interactions more powerful. Body language is more than just about the face. It involves the entire body working together. What do hand gestures have to do with this unspoken code? They are the primary tools that we use for many different purposes.

The actions of our hands send unsuspectingly messages. A person may bite their nails to indicate that they are anxious. It could be that they are trying to remove a damaged nail. This gesture, however, indicates anxiety and nervousness. Instead of biting your nails you might bite the end off a pen. The clenching of teeth can be a relief-inducing behavior.

Other gestures, such as tapping your fingertips on the table, are a sign of restless thoughts. Some people even go so far as to place their hands on their hips, sending signals of anxiety and anger.

There is a difference between nail biting, and holding your hands up to the hips. One gesture is more introverted than another. Hands on the hips, which are more confrontational, are more common. Unconsciously, we do this when trying to assertively speak. In a sense we are trying make ourselves larger and more powerful. How loud the nonverbal message will be depends on how the fingers and hands are placed. At ease, the hand will be more open and relaxed. When done in a threatening manner, the fingers will become more tightened and may even be clenched in one fist.

There are so many gestures and so few ways to interpret them. Hartland & Tosh (2001), authors of Guide to body language. The authors claim that there are over 700,000.000 body movements and positions related to nonverbal communications. This leaves a lot of interpretations.

Your hands hold almost a quarter the number of bones in your body. Each hand also has more than 30 muscles. It is obvious that our hands are used for more then just feeling and grasping.

Fingers

Our fingers can communicate many messages unsaid.

Different meanings can be attached to the gesture of pointing a fingers:

Pointing a finger may be used to point to the direction of someone in an attempt to help. This pointy finger gesture is loose and casual. Your other fingers could make a relaxed fist and have a relaxed thumb.

A person might point their finger at someone if they want to be aggressive or confrontational. The rigidity of the finger will enhance the shouting voice. The other fingers will become tighter together. Is the pointed tip a weapon or gun? It is often associated with an angry sound.

The way you poke your finger can have a dual meaning.

Aggression is the act of prodding another person using one finger, which can be stiff or poking hurtfully.

To push gently, rather than poke, is a less dangerous gesture.

There are a few messages that can be transmitted by the rhythm of your fingers. You can tell a lot about the drummer by the way they do it.

Drumming the fingertips fast can signify that the drummer has anxiety, is tense or is frustrated.

It is possible for a drummer to tap his fingers gently or more slowly when he thinks.

Even the thumb can transmit different messages.

Signs of appreciation or agreement include a loosely clenched thumb and thumb in an upwards orientation.

If your thumb is in a downwards-facing position, you send a negative message.

Hands

Our fingers are busy working as non-verbal communicators all day. The hand is typically only a part of complex nonverbal messages.

There will also be other body movements happening at the same time.

Hands and Shoulders

With your palms facing outward and your arms slightly raised, you can also shrug your shoulders. It's a quiet way of saying "I don't know", without having to use any words.

Face, Knees, and Hands

When praying, people will place their palms together, pray and then kneel with closed eyes, a closed mouth, and a relaxed appearance.

Hands, Fingers, Face

If you disagree with something, move your forefinger. How strongly you disagree will be evident by your facial expression.

Hidden Hands

You could hide your identity by putting your hands in your pockets. Your body language is not being understood by the other person. You're hiding one important indicator. Sometimes, your hands may be cold.

The number of gestures possible with hands is almost limitless. Hands are such an important communication tool, that people have even created sign language with their hands and fingers. This language does not require any words.

When understanding the strength and meaning of a hand signal, there are other movements that you need to be aware of. When someone does an insulting gesture with their finger, should they be doing it with just one or two fingers? It doubles the insult power by using two hands.

One researcher claims that scientists believe that spoken communication evolved from non-verbal gestures. He claims that these gestures not only enhance spoken language but play an essential role in it.

The fact that we can also touch and feel using our hands makes the hands an instrument of intimacy. Given the importance of our hands in our lives, it's no surprise that our hands are used for personal communications.

Arms

Your limbs can also communicate nonverbal messages. You can judge how someone feels about you by the way your arms and legs are positioned. We cross our arms defensively by crossing our arms, for example.

Usually, our arms will align with actions performed by our fingers and hands. We can cross our arms if we are upset or angered by someone. This creates a barrier between us. It's a completely unconscious process, as it often happens with body language. In frustration, it could be possible that we're trying to create a barrier. Depending on where we live, arm crossing can signify a variety of things.

It depends on the continent where you live that what message you are sending when you cross your legs. Crossing your legs can be a casual and easy process in the US. In Europe, however, it is more formal and structured.

Let's explore the science of body, limbs and nonverbal communication.

Barrier Or Boredom

As with any body language you need to learn how to place those unspoken messages in context. It's not because you are defensive or cross your arms when you are watching TV. The opposite is true. You're probably feeling relaxed and at peace. When you are reading body language, it is essential to also evaluate the surrounding environment.

If you are entertaining and the majority of the audience is not interested in your show, then you probably don't entertain very well.

We cross our arms often to defend ourselves against someone who upsets us.

But if you cross your arms as a sign that you are waiting for something or somebody, then this could be a sign you are bored.

It is not common for people to place their arms behind them. It may be uncomfortable. This could be because it exposes the front of your body, making you feel vulnerable. But there are exceptions. It is common for soldiers to stop marching and stand in this position as part their drill training. This is what they call "Standing at Ease". In this case, they are following orders and procedures instead of using unspoken language. However, it shows how uncommon it can be to stand in such a way.

This is possible for people who are more aware about their stance. As part of their training, soldiers may stop marching. Here, they are not following instructions but using a foreign language. However, it shows how unusual it can be to stand in this manner.

People who stand with their front exposed are showing confidence. This pose could even be considered arrogant, as they are expressing confidence that they have no fear. You can see this in the way they pose. If this is the case, the person will most likely have their hands relaxed behind their back and their shoulders open.

With our arms, we can send so many unspoken messages. These nonverbal messages are able to add to the spoken language or speak volumes for themselves.

Loud Or Quiet

An instinctual drive makes us gesture with our hands, arms, and hands to communicate. To make themselves appear larger, animals may use their appendages when they are attacked. Is this not what we are doing when we raise both our arms in the air? We could be communicating a message about how awesome we are or warning someone away like a threatening dog. This is another reason the environment matters. This could be as simple as waving your arms at someone to get their attention.

If the arms are flailing from the body, it is more like shouting our message. If we don't want our arms to be so prominent, we can move our arm-talk closer toward the body. Take a shrug of shoulders. Our hands might be used to send the silent message that "we don't have the answer". This gesture is more close to the body than if we want to shout that we don't know.

The majority of actions will be accompanied or complemented by other behaviors. It is possible to arm-wail with closed eyes. This is an extremely negative behavior. It could also be used to convey a loud message, such as "I don't really care." Like all body language, you will need to read more than one nonverbal act to determine the tone or meaning.

Elbows

The joint in our arms is also important. The aggressive posture of putting your hands on the hips is usually a sign that you are displaying aggression. It could be that we are trying to show off new clothes or encourage the opposite. The elbows make our bodies look larger. You might also be expanding your chest. That environment is key to determining the message.

You can use your elbows to boost your aggressive words. It is not a nice gesture to bend people in a crowd for you to pass, but they can be useful leverage tools with or without words.

They can be used to prop our heads up on our hands or lean the elbows against a table. This would be a great way to express how relaxed you are, without using words.

Chapter 5: It's Beat To The Eyes: Clues For Revealing True Intentions

Eye contact is a key indicator of neurological challenges in children. While this is not an easy thing to notice, it speaks volumes about the child's functioning. The social spectrum is high if a toddler can maintain direct eye contact at all times during their assessments. The lack of eye contact can be a sign of autism or social anxiety. The eyes are a window into our biology's inner workings.

What are you most likely to look at when meeting someone new? Most people's eyes show aspects of beauty that make them attractive in their first encounters. People often remember their eyes because of their shape, color and size. Neurotically, visual animals are programmed to make associations from what they see. These associations are generally defined by the energy we give off. The brain is responsible for every aspect of our bodies. How can our eyes communicate to certain receptors?

The Brain Meets The Eye

The retina acts like the gatekeeper to our attention. Through the exchange between sunlight and retina, all we see is transferred to the retina. Different neurons travel throughout our attention and communicate with different functions within it to receive unique signals. These signals are then carried by the nerves opticus into cerebral mantle. The cerebral brain is similar to the cinema. It controls our vision receptors that are responsible to perception, memory and thoughts. Researchers discovered that the pupil expands when our eye detects something pleasing. This is a proof that what we see will be what we anticipate. This will allow us to formulate opinions and draw conclusions. It also allows us to interpret our bodies' movements.

The eyes give certain clear signals that reveal true intentions.

Right glance: This is commonly used to forget about a person, a song or a reputation.

Left glance: This is used to recall visual stimulants such as texture, color and shape.

When in a correct position, you can look downward. This allows us to control our imaginations and determine what we think something should be.

Glancing down towards the left, Inner Communication, The Conversations We Have With Ourself

It is crucial to understand visual communication by understanding the way our eyes communicate with the brain. The eyes are an integral part of visual communication. We use every part in our bodies to communicate. To the untrained eye, the eyes might seem one-dimensional. The slight movements of the eyes can tell you everything you want to understand about a person. Let's examine a few examples.

Direct Eye Contact

Direct eye contact may indicate a feeling of discomfort. Self-confidence can be a good indicator that you're able to hold eyes. In order to be able to communicate awareness, recruiters will instruct interviewees to appear the interviewer when they interview them. This shows the interviewer that they aren't intimidated and will be able to tackle any task. In the same way, animals use eye contact to indicate dominance. Trainers will often look at their dog through the trainer's eyes to determine dominance. Dogs will be able to follow the commands of their trainer if they are locked eyes. Also, dominant signals are used by humans to communicate. Direct eye contact trumps fear. It shows you are open to the conversation and that you are interested in it.

Balance is the key ingredient to everything. Intense eye contact can make the recipient feel intimidated. An excessive stare could make other people feel uncomfortable. They might even question your ability to function. Imagine being able to have a conversation while looking at your eyes. Even when you looked away, they still had their eyes on you. You might have dismissed them as being extremely bizarre. You should always be aware of your eyes as staring can in some cultures be considered rude.

Looking Away

A sign of low self confidence is when someone avoids eye contact. They may be uncomfortable with the conversation, the person, or the environment they are in. People can be anxious about meeting new people in social settings. It can signal inner conflict if you avoid eye contact. It could be that they are resisting subconscious urges to attract and so avoid eye contact. This doesn't necessarily mean they are dishonest or untrustworthy. They will suffer from debilitating self consciousness that overwhelms their disposition.

Dilated Pupils

The pupils can generate complex signals that allow them to detect the smallest changes in their bodies. Study after study has shown that pupils who are faced with challenging questions grow in size. According to a 1973 study the pupils narrowen when their brains are challenged beyond its abilities. The brain's stress levels are also revealed in the eyes of pupils. So that they can see normal pupils, doctors will shine a little light in the eyes of their patients. If the pupils react well to the light and are of normal size, the brain shouldn't be in distress. A brain injury could be indicated by any imbalance.

As stated earlier, pupils who are dilate show extreme interest, and sometimes even agreement. When you hear or see something that sparks interest, your pupils will soon dilate. Similar results can be achieved when an individual is shown a representation they accept as true. In 1969, a respected researcher proved that pupils' dilation could indicate political affiliations. Participants became more interested in pictures of political figures that they admired and their eyes dilated. However, the pupils became narrower when shown a photo of a different political figure.

What Our Visual Directions Indicate

It is important to know where your eyes are located and what you specialize in during a conversation. A downward glance could signify shame, submission, and even shame. When children are being disciplined, they will often look down to express their disapproval for the child's behavior. One looked down in ancient Chinese culture when submitting to authority to show respect. Contrarily, looking up indicated arrogance. It is usually a sign of being bored or not wanting to get involved in the activity. Uncertainty is also signaled by looking up. A movie or tv show may feature an adolescent doing a test and looking up the answer because they aren't sure.

Sideways glances often indicate internal irritation. Inadvertently looking at people sideways is a sign of internal irritation. It can also happen when you're interacting with people that annoys you. The sideways stare can be translated into discontentment. When you notice something that's not right or someone sneaky, you'll give the side-eye. This is an expression of complete repulsion for their behavior, reputation, or perhaps their expressions.

Many believe squinting can be attributed to inability to determine. True, but a squint could also indicate disbelief. You may hear something you want to know more about. So they look at the speaker and squint their eyes. It's almost like they're saying, 'I don't believe'.

A person can become agitated by stress, which can cause rapid blinking. A person may be blinking rapidly and moving fast to complete a task. This could be caused by sweating or trembling. A subtle sign of arrogance might be excessive blinking. Excessive blinking, on the other hand, could be a sign of arrogance. For instance, a boss may flash his eyes while conversing with employees in an attempt to end their conversation. This blinking fast can effectively blind the worker from the boss for less than a second, which could be a sign that they are preferably doing something else.

If you have a direct stare and your lid is lowered, it's a sign of extreme attraction. It could be described as a "come-hither" invitation between partners. This gaze can be amplified through sexual attraction and should even induce pupil dilation.

Inability or inability to focus on the task at hand and a lack of ability to shine a light

An eye nystagmus measures how long it takes a person's body to focus on one more point while undergoing extreme movements. An individual who displays a prolonged nystagmus (more than 14 seconds) will have problems staying focused. One academic facility tests the accuracy a child's ability to nystagmus by spinning them a number of times and asking them to look up towards the ceiling. The pupils then respond by moving rapidly, sometimes dilation then narrowing. The time it takes for the kid's eyes to stabilize is recorded. They continue spinning weekly in the hopes of increasing their focus and ability to remain focused on one task despite being distracted by many things. As they gain a tolerance, their vision will stabilize even if they are not using as much of your time. This is done to improve their ability to reject outward distractions, which can help with attentive deficit disorder. The movements of the eyes can tell trained professionals in which area and how much assistance a toddler requires. Aren't the eyes amazing?

Our eyes can reveal many aspects of ourselves. You are ready to gain psychological insight on your perception of yourself and others. With a simple glance If you pay close attention, you can often detect irritation, lust and attraction. Because the eyes are the first link to the brain, it is only natural that they are also the gatekeepers of the soul. This will give you the ability to investigate complex individuals by incorporating these simple tips into your everyday life. It is also possible to detect deceit using the eyes. We will soon learn how the eyes reveal trustworthiness in privates as we continue our visual communication adventure.

Chapter 6: Be Aware Of Emotional Energy

Emotional energy can be described as a form or energy that we all have. It's expressed through our verbal, non-verbal cues. Everybody can sense and experience emotion energy. This is a widely used communication tool that allows people to communicate important information. People can use emotional communication to make connections or protect themselves. Depending on what is happening, emotional communication can help groups to identify and address a problem.

You can also use your intuition to read energy, as with all other forms. However, you can also read emotions in other ways. Knowing how to read the emotional energy of a person will enable you to rely on intuition and your knowledge to make an accurate reading. This allows you to get a better reading and can then use it to your advantage.

Sense People's Presence

Everyone can feel the energy of people who are present in their space. A great way to identify this is to think back to when a friend last visited your home. It's possible to feel their energy within your home. Because your home is where you spend a lot, it is easy to detect changes in the energy. It is also possible to sense their presence by imagining the difference in energy between two people, like Charles Manson and Dalai Lama.

Everyone has a certain energy that they exude when they are present. It pays well to find out what that energy is whenever you meet someone. Pay close attention the energy that people exude and how it affects your feelings. It is important to notice if people feel happy, cheerful, and enjoy being around them. These indicate which energy archetypes they are likely to have.

Pay Attention To Their Eyes

The age-old expression, "Eyes can reveal a person's heart", is true. Your eyes are a powerful tool for expressing love, hate, or other strong emotions. The brain sends electromagnetic signals through its eyes, which can be picked up by other people. This energy can be felt whenever you feel someone staring back at you, even though they were not initially looking at you.

Look into the eyes of a person to determine their emotions. Pay close attention to the type of looks they give back. Trust your intuition but keep an eye out for other clues. If they don't look at me, this could indicate that they are unhappy or angry with you. If they gaze deeply into your eyes and feel that you are loved, understood, and valued, they will know you have an energy of compassion. If you feel unwelcome, uncomfortable or hunted you may be in the company of someone who doesn't have your best interests at heart. If you trust your intuition, you will be able to discern the true meaning of someone's glance.

Feel their Physical Touches

Persons' physical touch communicates a lot about their feelings. Handshakes are the most common touchpoints. Every touch-based experience can send you significant amounts of energy. Pay attention.

Handshakes, which are a form touch, can be shared with anyone. A simple handshake can give you important information. You can see if the person is nervous, anxious, confident, engaged, disinterested, outgoing, or withdrawn. You can tell a lot by the way a person is expressing themselves around a handshake. If a person looks at you, leans in front of you, has their hands on yours, or points toward you, they're engaged and enjoying the conversation. They will not be interested in communicating if they are uninterested or neutral.

Hugs can convey a lot. This is an indication that a person feels friendly to you but not like they are close. The pat signifies that they feel uncomfortable, and they may not know the right expression to express their feelings. A person who hugs you from the behind indicates that they view you as a lover. However, it is only shared between lovers. Hugging from behind is a sign that the person is feeling protective and wants to show you how much their love. A tight hug from a person to you, especially when it turns into an embrace means that they are showing you they care. A-frame Hugs are hugges where a person offers you a tight hug out of obligation, and not because they want to. The rest of their body is kept away from you, with the exception of their shoulders.

Random acts or touching can occur, even though they aren't expected nor necessary. You might feel someone touch your arm or leg while talking to you. As we are more aware of who is around us, touching is almost never accidental. If we don't want it to, we will not touch or physically connect with them. If someone contacts you, it is usually because they want. This almost always indicates that the person cares about you and is engaged in your situation. These gestures can be interpreted as a sign that someone cares or wants you to feel better. You may not notice the gestures if they seem random, but it could indicate that they care about you.

Intentional touch is more common among lovers. It is likely that you have experienced touch from your partner many times. You can determine a change in their emotions by the change in their touch. You can tell if someone is feeling disengaged or not wanting to have any physical contact by their touch. You may notice your partner doing this when they feel stressed or have had a rough day. If your partner feels more comfortable touching you than usual, they may want to feel closer to the two of you. If you have any questions, you can always ask your partner for their thoughts, feelings, or needs.

Listen to their Tone, and Laugh

Based solely on their tone, you can quickly tell if someone has fake laughter or communication. Genuine laughter and tone of voice will emanate from someone who is grounded and genuine. Their laughter and tone will be hearty and full. They may sound hollow, empty, forced, or fake it to hide what they really feel and think.

Emotions such as sadness, anger and low confidence can be detected in the voice of a person. It is easy to pick up different emotions just by listening to their tone or how they are speaking. This form of hearing is best when you listen to many emotions. You can then truly hear the differences between them. Sometimes they are subtle and difficult to explain. Listening to recordings of people who express many emotions is a great way for you to get used to hearing their emotions. Check to see if each emotion is correctly identified. This will help you pick up emotional energy from people's laughs and voices.

Sense Your Heart Energy

Each person has their heart energy which can be used to bring out the best in others or withdraw from them. Feeling full around someone who has their heart energy is a sign of a person's true self. They behave and communicate in ways that show that they are fully themselves and are deeply committed to the present moment. It is easy to sense if a person isn't bringing their heart energy. Some people just feel "off" or "missing." People who know someone well will quickly be able tell if their heart isn't in it. However, those who have just met them may need patience as they learn to interpret their unique energy.

It is easy to tell that some people are not invested in what they do and say. It is important to pay more attention when dealing with other people. Are you able to feel their positive intentions, unconditional love, warmth and warmth as they move through the day? Is it possible that they are frustrated or annoyed by the tasks they have been assigned? People with great heart energy are more likely to express passion and peace even if they're doing something they hate. It is their deepest nature that they are passionate and peaceful. Those who are unable to express their emotions during stressful times or in disappointment may not be being authentic and may not be communicating the truth. They may not know how or act authentically if they are completely disconnected from their heart. To understand their true intentions and messages, pay more attention.

Chapter 7: Body Language In Sell

Although you could give the best speech, nobody will ever remember you if all you do is speak in whispers with a darkened expression while you deliver your speech. As important as the delivery of the speech is how it is delivered to the audience. What you say makes more sense than what it says. While the speech is important, it is less important than the delivery of the speech. How you deliver the speech, what the words sound like, and how the people are listening to it, are all important. It is important that you pay attention not only to what is being said, but also how your body and eyes are aligned. When selling policy or anything you want people to profit from, this matters to both the audience as well as to you. A good non-verbal communication skill is more important than your body language. This allows you to capitalize on the situation, manipulate and control the audience. A persuasive body language communicates the same message and influence. The way it is integrated to mean the exact same thing is crucial in this concept.

By using body language, one can strategically emphasize the argument to get their attention and engage them in the entire issue of engagement. Your goal is to get your client to understand the products and your business. It is crucial to be able to communicate with your potential clients in a way that appeals to them. Otherwise, you may lose their attention or fail to make the intended sales. This form of communication is crucial for communication. Producers, sellers, and intermediaries must take this seriously, especially in business settings. To communicate an important point to your audience, you can move towards them, smile, nod, maintain eye contact, and nod. These gestures can create a positive atmosphere for the audience as well as confidence.

One can increase the confidence when presenting by opening arms and chest, while keeping a straight back. This position helps one breathe clearly while delivering the speech. It is possible to build trust with the audience by giving the best presentation. It can be a friendship that is built, which leads to increased sales. The only way to give your business an edge in the marketplace is by overcoming sales challenges.

In sales, the attitude we have will determine the outcome of the negotiations. How much we discuss is a direct reflection on how we feel about it. The challenges are all around us and we must learn to transcend them. Having that in mind will help us to make a positive impression with body language, as well as our overall appearance. The same old boring business call does not change things. However, the attitude we have in our tone can make a difference.

Engaging the eyes rather than looking at them in a boring gaze can convert people to your way of thinking and can help them focus on what they are trying to convey. It is a sign that you are paying attention to what they are saying and that you trust their ideas. But, you should be careful not overdo it as this could mean that your stare is strangely creepy to others. You should smile when you speak. This relaxes the muscles, making it more attractive. You create a welcoming smile that helps the other person feel appreciated and loved, no matter what kind of relationship they have. But be mindful not to exaggerate your smile. A deceiving smile can make conversation dull and boring. It is also important that you take into consideration the behavior of the other party when selling.

Selling is a stressful business. It can lead to you biting your lip, chewing your nails, pulling your hair out and tearing your hair. You can have good, rolling fun once you master its flow and understand its parry to commercial life. How one sees deals and the importance of connecting with others is key. One cannot sell personal items without having a connection. If you don't have that, your business might not work for you. It is important to remember that people are only able to feel valued, desired and loved by those they love. In business, personal selling and other areas, it is difficult to achieve that level of importance, love, and admiration. Everyone wants to be appreciated, desired and loved by others. Even politicians love the psychopaths who praise others everywhere they go. The ones who praise and name them are the ones who are most valued by these people. It is impossible to win the sales pitch if you don't believe your client is worthy, valuable and capable of meeting your needs. Although this sounds scary, it is the truth. People must always accept and be open to accepting the truth in order succeed in any business dealing.

One should try to look at the speaker whenever they are sharing their ideas. This shows that both of you are at the same level. You are aware what their feelings are, how they perceive the whole idea. It is important to maintain a positive gaze and appeal to the speaker in order to avoid negative feelings.

The speaker will be able to understand your concern if you keep the gaze open. You are permitted to express your concern. However, it is important to remember the speech of the speaker before you do so. This will make them feel valued, loved, and well understood.

All things considered, however, the level of comprehension, understanding, and general perceptions of the ideas is determined by the body language that the speaker uses during the speech. One should not hesitate to say "Thank you" while speaking. It gives off a positive energy that makes the speaker feel good and like they are winning the battle. The nodding conveys that you are sympathetic, grateful, and interested in others' ideas.

If someone is speaking, leaning forward can indicate that you are not trying to invade their territory. If you move closer to someone who is speaking, it shows you are interested and willing to listen. It doesn't matter how casual or formal your conversation with them will be. What is important is how you present yourself to them. How ready you are, in order to receive their full attention during speaking. This gesture is great for gaining respect from clients in business settings where attentiveness and respect are highly valued. If you are engaging in a lively conversation that requires attention, you can assist by using an open hand gesture. You should let the other person know you are doing it unconsciously, and not forcing it to happen. You can feel the enthusiasm that comes from such gestures, and it will show in your actions.

To make sales, your body language should be consistent with the speaker's speech. The speech must be able to convey the audience's emotions and perceptions. In most cases, you will need to deliver a speech before a large audience. If this is the case, then be ready to capitalize on the opportunity to benefit from it. Doing so will allow you to attract more positivity, which will result in a positive perception. It is possible to mirror such events in order to create a vision of the future and a desire to achieve your set goals. It's similar to having a clear plan for achieving your set goals and objectives in life and business. This strategy plan gives you a competitive advantage in your market. In this instance, the market refers to the desired goal that other competitors have in mind. There must be an intention to every conversation. In order for things to work out your way, you should have clear goals. You also need to make sure the other person understands them by using a persuasive speech pattern. It can be a sign that you're putting too much pressure on the other person when you speak too fast. It can also indicate that you aren't interested or concerned enough about the subject at hand if you speak too slow. You can practice by mirroring this before you deliver the speech. This will enable you to see how your speech will turn out.

It is interesting to notice that people can be more positive if they remain calm when they are giving a speech. It will show that you are listening and agreeing with the speaker's words. The crowd will feel more connected to the speaker and feel better knowing that someone is listening. You might be wondering why some people prefer to talk while keeping their mouths shut. Why do they prefer nodding rather than answering any questions that are thrown at them. It is fascinating to see how it affects people. Talking to them allows them to express their thoughts, fears, and feelings. Listening is a way to make them feel loved, valued and appreciated by the listener. Even if your bar of gold has a higher price than everyone else, you can still master the art and skill of listening. If you do this, you will likely win their trust and friendship which could lead to a long-lasting partnership. Connectivity built through friendship is all that's needed in business. It is important to be careful when engaging in such relationships. It might seem less important to one person, but it is very important to the other.

You should always be careful when you shake hands. What matters is how you behave when handing out that crucial handshake. It doesn't matter how much pressure you put into it. Handshakes that are meant for women don't necessarily work for men. It doesn't work that way. Women prefer a warm, caring handshake. Men need to be able to give pressured handshakes. When you shake hands with men, it is important to do it right. Otherwise, it could sell you out or worsen things.

Chapter 8: Nonverbal Cues For The Torso

For the torso we can see that the limbic mind will with great diligence instruct us to safeguard this part of our bodies. Not only is the torso more vulnerable to serious injuries, but it also houses several vital organs, such as the heart, liver, stomach, and lungs.

The brain senses danger regardless of whether it is real or imagined. It automatically sends a message through the torso to ensure that internal organs are protected from harm.

This is the primary way we can decode nonverbal trunk cues. The 'torso Lean' and torso Shield' are the two main ones.

The Torso Lean

Just like the rest your body, your torso will first react to danger by creating distance between it and the danger. If someone throws a missile at your body, you will instinctively try to dodge it. A person who is close to an annoying person will naturally lean away.

It is easy for you to notice the relationship between two people just by looking at their torsos. They will likely share a great connection and relationship, if they sit together and are open to ventral facing each other.

The Torso Shield

People will try to cover their torsos with something, but you can almost feel the discomfort.

Men will use torso shielding in subtle ways, possibly because they have stronger, more muscular bodies. A man might pull at his shirt sleeves, fuss with his tie, or lightly scratch the chin. These are subtle protections that communicate that the man feels uneasy.

Women will protect their torsos in more obvious ways, however. A woman will often cross her arms over her stomach to protect her torso.

The last tip: Men should not panic if they are going on a first date with a woman who exhibits such nonverbal behavior. It does not necessarily mean that she is unwilling to be with you. You may find that she is intimidated by your appearance, especially if she is older or more experienced and believes that hurting or rejection is possible. Asking them to high-five is a great way to get rid of this feeling. This moves promotes good feelings while showing the torso.

Let's now understand the arms.

Nonverbal cues of the arms

When it comes to assessing nonverbal behavior, the arm is a little under-appreciated. People rely on facial expressions and other nonverbal cues to understand the reason behind an individual's actions and reactions. The arms however can provide significant information regarding a person's actions.

The theory is that arms weren't necessary for movement in the evolution of humans and were therefore able to be used to aid us in other ways.

Arms are useful for many purposes, including lifting heavy items and launching us off of the ground. They also provide defense and other functions. They can be responsive when threats are presented because they have the freedom to move their arms and hands.

The two most important nonverbal cues to the arms that are not verbal are the'regal stance' or the 'arms-akimbo'.

The Regal Stance

This is the position where we place our arms behind us. Consider the noblemen you see in movies, especially when they are speaking to others.

This move is frequently associated with people who are high-status and often observed. It is a move that indicates distance and the desire to attain this distance to convey personal worth.

This move can be misinterpreted. It communicates that the person 'owning' it doesn't enjoy being touched. It is well-known that people feel unworthy of touching, and this is a problem because human touch is essential for our interaction.

This being said, we humans have learned to use touch as a gauge of our current feelings. Arm-distancing can lead to discomfort. When this happens, we tend avoid those objects that we dislike. As a baby's diaper, you will probably dispose it as quickly and with as few fingers possible.

Arms Akimbo

Our arms might be used as territorial-marking tools. However, despite our advanced social nature, human beings are territorial creatures at their core. Established territory and protecting it were a matter of life and loss hundreds of thousand of years ago. The human mind, as he evolved, has never lost sight.

The most powerful and potent territorial projection is the arms akimbo. This is when your arms are wrapped around your waist. It may be used for dominance, confidence, communication, or even to raise an issue.

If someone is addressing you and they adopt this posture, it is likely that they have an issue or are getting agitated and will soon get confrontational.

Nonverbal cues of the Fingers, Hands and Fingers

In terms of their ability to accomplish so many tasks, all animal species have hands. But the human hand is the only one. Each invention that required attention and concentration was created by the hands and fingers. Hands can grab, grasp and poke, scratch, punch, sense, perceive, assess and mold the environment and its contents.

You can also use them to express your feelings. Hands bring an intensity and edge to conversations. They are great tools to help others understand the messages that we have for them.

The hands can certainly betray intents and can reflect subtle behavioral nuances.

We will analyze two powerful hand movements: "steeping and hand-wringing", "thumb display" and others.

Hand Steeping and hand-wringing

Hand steepling, one of the strongest signs of confidence, is a sign that you are confident. Steeping means to touch the fingers of both hands together, but not in an interlaced fashion. The palms should not touch one other.

It is also known as steepling. Because it resembles a church steeple's top, the gesture is often called steepling. It indicates that you have great confidence in yourself and that your thoughts and position are well-aligned.

Steeping is used to give you the ability to deliver your message and also to command attention.

On the other side, hand-wringing is a sign that you are feeling uneasy and uncomfortable. Hand wringing, where the fingers interlace as though making a prayer gesture, is what you do. It's amazing to see how quickly someone can switch between steepling and hand wringing within a matter of seconds. This is an indication that you are experiencing a change in your mood or reaction to something they just said or did.

These two gestures can be understood by watching as many debates and listening to as many as possible. Debates are often a place of high mental pressure. You will see people switching from steepling to hand wringing quite frequently.

Thumb Displays

The thumb is the most distinctive finger. It is unique and one of the most essential fingers.

We would be living in the Stone Age without our thumbs. It is so important that we don't have to use all of its tiny movements and twists. This is how you can really understand the power behind the thumb. Since the dawn of time, thumbs have been a significant way for people to express their feelings.

The thumbs-up sign communicates positivity and approval. In addition, subconsciously, the thumbs-up signalling confidence and relaxation is sent when you place your hands in your pocket.

If you are tucking the thumbs in your pockets with the rest, this could be a sign that you are having negative emotions or that your edge is high. It could also be a sign that the temperature is below 30, so you need to enjoy warmth whenever possible.

I am sure that you are familiar with body language and have the ability to read feet and arms to determine what someone is trying to communicate. To be a "guru", it helps to understand deceptive language. The following chapters will discuss this topic in greater detail.

Chapter 9: Reading People

It is possible to assume that you have some genuine curiosity about your fellow humans. This is vital in learning how people can be analysed effectively. To be able to effectively analyze people, it is essential to approach them with a positive, curious and objective outlook. Listen carefully and observe how they behave and look. Then, analyze the information you have heard and seen to determine if there is a pattern to their personality.

For reliable analysis of people, you'll need to be able to follow four rules:

* Remain objective

* Watch out for congruent patterns

* Read body language and voice in clusters

* Pay attention the context

Look at the clusters to understand body language, voice, overall appearance.

People make a very common and easy mistake when starting to analyze people. They take one single piece of information, and extrapolate a person's personality based on it. A salesman might scratch their head and talk to you about insurance. It is a mistake to assume that this means that the salesman is lying. Head scratches can take many different meanings. You might think the salesman is forgetful. He may have lice. You can't get a good read on someone if you only look at one indicator.

It is useful to view human analysis in the same way as learning another language. People constantly exchange nonverbal messages.

As with any language, nonverbal communication uses punctuation, words and sentences. Every gesture and inflection should be viewed as a word within the sentence. Each word can have multiple meanings.

To give you an example, I would like to know what your response would be to a question about the meaning of "set". The meaning of "Set" can take on over 4000 different meanings depending on its context. Therefore, you will probably need more information before giving a definitive definition. For any word to have any type of reliability in meaning, it is necessary to put them into sentences.

Also, nonverbal messages are also conveyed in a type we'll call "clusters". As you need at minimum three words in English to make a sentence and then interpret it correctly, you should never analyze someone until you have accounted for at least three pieces. First, pay attention to what your body language and voice are telling you. Next, look at how the person looks. Once you have the three components of your "sentence", you can match the nonverbal group with the actual words used by the person to reach a reliable conclusion.

Pay attention to context

Any communication must be interpreted within its environment or context to ensure accuracy. As a scatterplot, think about points.

The scatter plot would only have one dot. This would mean that you wouldn't know which direction the trend was moving. This principle also applies to humans.

Imagine a person sitting down, with their arms crossed and their head down.

Consider also the possibility that the person is shaking his/her leg very quickly, speaking in an inconsistent tone, rhythm and avoids eye contact.

This person could be liar if the police were to interrogate him. But, if this person is waiting outside a bus stop in winter, it is more likely they are cold.

The person sitting in a hospital waiting room is not likely to be lying or cold, but they may be anxious or ill. If you asked me what tattoos mean for a mid-twenty man, I would not be able answer you without additional information. If the tattoo shows that the man is in the armed services, then he might be a conformist. A person who works in an office might be rebellious. Perhaps he is trendy if he plays in a band. A temporary tattoo might be possible if he is at the carnival with his children.

It is important that you understand the context of nonverbal communication.

Every aspect of an individual's vocal quality, words, and body language is subject to many interpretations. Therefore, you will need a way to interpret each one in the light of the particular circumstances.

Which they do. When you analyze, don't forget context.

Stay Objective

Without objective analysis, you cannot accurately assess people. Ironically, the more significant the conclusion, the harder it is to stay objective because of the emotion involved.

Furthermore, people often make decisions based upon what they believe will be best for them now, and not on rational considerations of all the evidence. To avoid negative experiences, the human mind tends not to recognize truths it finds as dangerous.

Leon Festinger described this tendency of the mind not to accept unpleasant realities as cognitive dissonance. It accounts for the majority of loss in objectivity.

For you to be objective, it is important to forget your instinct to avoid facts that upset you. It is easy to understand what causes you distress and why. You will be better equipped to react to these triggers.

Reduced objectivity can often be caused by four mental states. When we are being: We lose our objectivity.

* Defensive

*

* Emotionally attached

Defensive

We often shut down in defense of perceived threats when we feel attacked or criticised. When we do that, our better judgement goes out the window.

We can't defend ourselves while maintaining objectivity simultaneously. Ironically it is precisely when you feel attacked and criticized that it is the most crucial time to keep your objectivity.

If you feel defensive or lose your objectivity and become defensive, remember that there will be a place and time for you to speak your mind in the future. Your response will be more effective if now you have taken the time to consider and fully understand what you will be responding too. It is best to let go of all defensiveness and keep your ears, eyes, and mind open for what is before you.

It is necessary

Feeling like you need something from someone makes other considerations fall down our priority list.

One of those considerations includes objectivity.

For example, people are more likely to avoid grocery stores when they are hungry. They fear their hunger will make them unwise. The same principle applies when analyzing people. If you are in a position to quickly determine if someone is lying, this could be an example. In your rush to decipher truth, you could make poor judgments about the person. If you find yourself reacting differently to the issue than you would if there was more time, it is likely that you are too needy. You will lose your objectivity and be less accurate in reading people. It is important that you pause at these moments to think about alternative motivations.

Emotionally Attached

Human beings can be stubborn. We aren't willing to look down on the people we love. And we don't want any good in the people that we hate.

Furthermore, most people hate change. A lot of our emotional stability is dependent upon maintaining the status-quo. Also, it is important to keep the belief system that those we love are beautiful, and that those we dislike are evil.

An emotional attachment to maintaining equilibrium can lead to a loss of objectivity regarding those closest to us. The rule of thumb is that the more emotional attachment we have, the more likely our brains are to engage with irrational analysis. You need to be careful not to analyze people emotionally and not objectively.

You can avoid situations where you may feel pressured or coerced to make a decision. It will only lead to your objectivity being eroded. It is also important not to voice your opinion about anyone to others until you have taken enough time to get the relevant information.

Avoid revealing your conclusions prematurely. This is because once people make a public commitment to an opinion, they won't be willing to change that view. People are generally resistant to change.

In the event that you start to analyze people closest to you but don't have enough time to do so or you are unable think critically or gather additional information, your ability for objective thinking is likely to decrease. Simply take note of what you feel and put them aside while you analyze the individual. Although you may not be able remove that annoying emotion, it is possible to at least control it.

Congruent patterns are worth your attention

Studies have shown that fivety-five percent of communication can be described as nonverbal. This includes body language and appearances, thirty-eight% vocal communication (how statements were made), and around seven percent verbal communication (what is being said). Nonverbal communication can carry six times as much weight than words actually spoken. This is important because it shows that when spoken words are not in agreement with nonverbal signs, the observer will almost always follow the nonverbal message. This is especially true when it comes to women. This is because people often stop listening when they don't understand what the other person is saying.

Imagine that someone is interviewing candidates for a job. Their arms are folded tight and their neck is down. While they talk about their "people skills," the candidate is seated back in their chair.

The body language of the candidate would suggest someone who is closed off and defensive, critical, critical, and potentially hostile. While their words try to convey an opposite impression, it could be interpreted as such.

In this situation, the interviewer would rely on the candidate's nonverbal cues to establish that the candidate was not very friendly. Any type of accurate analysis will require the ability to recognize patterns and clusters in nonverbal cues.

It is important to understand the nonverbal information of a person when analysing them.

It is then necessary to examine all of the information to see if there are any patterns that reveal reliable facts. These patterns are called:

* Consider the most obvious characteristics of the person to be your baseline. Then, compare what you learn with the baseline.

Look out for exaggerated features. How suppressed or exaggerated a trait might affect how important it is.

* Look for inconsistencies or ambiguities in the pattern.

* You should consider whether the state you are observing can be considered a permanent trait or temporary.

* *Differentiate between voluntary and non-voluntary characteristics. Some traits can't be controlled. Others can be controlled.

* Prioritize high-predictive traits.

Start with the obvious

There are three main layers to information you want to learn about an individual.

The most basic layer of information available to the intelligent people-reader is the objective and general. It includes information like the person's marital status as well as their job, hobbies, and favorite T.V. It includes information about the person's education, age, and how many and what kind of children they have.

This second layer of information is subjective. It is based more on what you can physically observe and how it is perceived. This could include the person's body language, the relevance and importance of specific actions, and vocal attributes. It will take a broad understanding of what the person's most obvious features mean to you in order to get this information.

The third layer is the one in which you draw conclusions using the information that you have gathered from the first two layers. Is the person meticulous or lazy? Do they act passively or aggressively? Rude or polite Are you introverted, or are you extroverted

Note the top three to four traits that you notice when you meet someone new. This analysis will give a first impression about a person. Be aware that these impressions are just the impressions you had from the person at first. It is important to continuously measure any additional information beyond your first impression in order to identify patterns. Also, pay particular attention to any information that contradicts your first impression. You might come up with a different conclusion if you find inconsistencies.

Exaggerated Characters

The importance of any trait directly correlates with its subtlety, size, intensity, and smallness.

In other words, it is difficult to judge the importance and significance of a trait. Once you've learned enough about someone to recognize a pattern, however, you won't be able accurately assess the significance of any trait. Look out for other traits or characteristics that match the most dramatic. If you look at an obese man, it is possible to assume that he is self conscious about his weight. However, if you talk with him and notice that his body language is open and that he uses a loud voice to communicate emotions, it may be necessary to revise what impression you had.

Look out for Inconsistency

An individual's personality or unusual traits can be significant. There are two categories of deviations.

The first type of deviation includes traits that are inconsistent with others. These traits will be called "rebel genes".

The second kind of deviation is any behavior that isn't in line with an individual's regular routine or habits. These actions are called "rebel activities".

If you discover a rebel trait, you need to investigate it.

When the person has managed to conceal every other clue, sometimes the rebel trait gives a glimpse of the person's true nature.

But, often, the outlying personality allows you to gain some insight into someone's inner workings, rather than their veracity. If a business person is a confident and professional, it would be because they are organized, conservative, and well-dressed. A bracelet that was handmade by the child of this individual would indicate a rebel trait.

This would indicate that this person isn't just a professional with a great attitude, but is also very attached to his family.

Rebel actions, however, can be more revealing than rebel attributes. We are all creatures that follow routines and have established habits. Unless something unexpected happens, we will usually stick to our normal routines. If your neighbor becomes increasingly agitated and starts to ignore you, then you'll know that something is wrong.

Asking your spouse to stop calling you late at night to let you know they are not working is a good idea. Don't get too paranoid. Although a slight deviation from your usual routine shouldn't be considered a problem, it should alert you to the fact that you need to pay more attention. You will gain a greater understanding of the character of an individual regardless of their motivations.

Temporary state or permanent trait?

When trying to find a pattern it is important that you distinguish between temporary emotions or behaviours and more permanent ones. Each saint has a story, and even devils can quote scripture for their own purposes. This is to say that while bad people may do evil things sometimes, good people often do good things. As with all aspects of an analysis of people, single incidents are rarely indicative of a person's true nature. If you're trying to find a pattern in someone's behavior, you need to be able to tell if this is an isolated event or if it is part of a bigger pattern.

Chapter 10: Understanding Body Language

BODY-LANGUAGE ATTRACTION

Body language is an essential element of fascination. When discussing love, dating and sentiments, body language plays an important role.

So many people wonder:

"What took place in this relationship?"

"Do they like you?"

"Why didn't he call?"

You can use body language to find out where you stand.

The question is, how can we use body language to make ourselves alluring? How does body language play a role in fascination?

It's quite amazing to discover that cave dwellers had a similar body language. This body language is now vastly enhanced. Here are some messages you can send with your body to show an interest in someone else:

*I am open

*I'm innocuous

*I'm intrigued

*I'm friendly

*I'm prolific

The question is: How can fascination be achieved?

Helen Fisher, Rutgers University Anthrologist, states that the body is able to instantly detect if someone is physically attractive. These are body language signals that people typically find attractive.

* Accessibility: Both women and men find individuals with accessible bodylanguage the most attractive. Accessible bodylanguage is grinning and uncrossed hands, upward

looking (not looking at shoes or telephones), and smiling.

* Fertility. This is a transformative view. People can be tuned into body language prompts which flag youth and fruitfulness. These signs can be underlined by body language. Men can indicate their fruitfulness by standing straight up, squaring their shoulders, showing hands, and putting your feet slightly wider than shoulder width apart. To attract a woman, you can hold your hair down, tilt your head to reveal pheromones, and expose your wrists and hands to show the delicate skin.

BODY LANGUAGE YE CONTACT

The body communicates feelings through its exterior appearance. Different states of mind can be created by blending the eyes, eyebrows and nose. You may be upbeat or pitiful, discouraged or angry.).

A couple is trying to show the difference between their outer appearance and their inner expressions (i.e. The non-verbal communication method is consistent when it comes to deciphering our feelings. Studies of behavioral analysis have shown that an acknowledgement of outward appearance may be affected by the expression of the face. This indicates that cerebrums form facial and substantial expressions for all other subjects. In these reviews, subjects demonstrated accuracy in judging feelings from their outer appearance. This is because the body, as well as the face, are normally observed in equal amounts. The passionate signs coming from the face and body are highly coordinated.

BODY LANGUAGE OF LOYALITY

Did you ever wish that there were an enchantment tool you could use to make yourself more attractive to the inverse of sex? If so, how would you be able to understand what makes someone pull you into them? It's not a magic wand, but it is a science. Here are some ways that men and women can excel in the field of adoration.

"Body Language is hardwired within our brains and subsequently used as a component of oblivious development," says Allan Pease. He is the creator of The Body Language of Love. "Ladies have better wiring for getting on nonverbal signs so if men wish to increase their chances of mating diversion they need to learn how to translate signals females use."

BODY-LANGUAGE GESTURES

Movements can be defined as movements that are made with parts of the body (e.g. These movements can be performed with hands, arms or fingers. A few different ways can you decode arm signals. When someone stands, walks, or sits in a conversation with their arms collapsed, it is usually not a good sign. This could suggest that they are closed-minded and unable to listen to the speaker. Another form of arm movement includes an arm traversing another, which can indicate instability and a lack of certainty.

Hand movements are a sign of prosperity. Gripped hands can indicate anxiety or stress, while loose hands signify confidence and ease. This could be an indication of anxiety and apprehension if a man is grasping his hands.

In addition to being used to indicate one's talk, finger signals also represent the state of the person who makes them. Certain societies consider guiding with one's pointed finger to be worthy. However, the act of pointing at men might be considered forceful in other societies. For example, Hindus may consider it hostile to point at men. Instead, they point with the thumbs. In the US, France and Germany, thumbs up signals could also be used. However, the same signal can offend in different countries such as Iran and Bangladesh.

The Head Nod can be used in many societies to express understanding or "Yes". It is a type of hindered bowing, where the individual does not bow but instead holds back and makes the gesture. The Head Nod signifies that we are accepting the perspective of another person. Bowing, on the other hand, is an easygoing signal. Directed with people who are visually impaired, hard of hearing or stupid, this motion is often used to suggest 'Yes'. This creates the impression of an unalienable signal that accommodation is possible.

FLIRTING BODY LANGUAGE

Body language is an essential component of being a tease. It highlights sexual contrasts and is what makes a man appealing to other people. Dr. Albert Scheflen states that physiological changes happen when men meet someone they're occupied with.

The body expects a more upright stance and muscle tone, which makes the individual appear more youthful and attractive.

A man will stand taller and open his trunk to appear more intense. But a woman will tilt her head and touch the hair of her lady while uncovering her wrists. Your body language can show you how friendly, charming, energetic, or even fiercely independent you are.

There are a few signs that a tease body language shows. These signs are subtle and unobserved, but others are deliberate and carefully observed. The center standard of tease body language is underlining sexual differences so as to draw in the reverse sex. These distinctions are what make a man "provocative" and attractive.

Multiple studies into romance showed that most women initiate sentimental experiences 90% of the times. They do it by sending simple gestures such as body flags and eye-, face-, or body flags to their male counterparts.

If a man had the shrewdness to read the signs, he would approach them. While some men do approach women with no signs sent, there are few who will. Their success rate with romance is lower because they are more likely to get closer to women than men. Surprisingly it isn't true in 90% of relationships. Men are not the ones who make the first move.

In truth, men have trouble understanding subtle signs of the feminine body language and are unable to effectively translate them. They can have as much as 10 to 20 times the testosterone of ladies and mix their neighborly grins up with sexual intrigue.

Even though this is not a common practice, many women find it amusing to send negating signals to their man when they are actually interested. This allows women to get to know the man. Some men will be confused by this conflicting data and may not want to make their approach at all, regardless of how the signs are being communicated.

POSITIVE BODY LANGUAGE

When I talk about positive body language, it means that I mean being open, curious and friendly, rather than the guarded, guarded type of body language I spoke about earlier. However, it doesn't mean you need to use it all the time. Instead, this should be a set of signs that convey a positive and congenial state of mind.

This can be something to be thankful. Let's try to see how we can make others open up to us, and create trust by showing consideration.

KEEP AWAY DARING BARRIERS

In order to build trust with others, we need to show them that we aren't a risk and that we don't fear them. Protective body language has an impact on our mentality. It's not uncommon for people to avoid us when we're stressed.

The process of warming up to someone is not an easy one. Don't worry if they aren't willing to open up at your first attempt. If you are interested in the other person, you can speed-up the "warming down" process or, if possible, get to know their general attitude towards you.

Expect someone to cross their body when they meet you for the first time. If they do, expect them to keep a good distance from each other. This is also a sign of discomfort or unfamiliarity. As relations become more comfortable, the leg boundary will diminish and they may be closer to each other.

Then, they will start to move more quickly and reveal their palms. The person may then move more easily and their arms may not cross. You should also watch out for a person's tendency to lean in towards yours by inclining their body.

We subconsciously copy the body language around us. Inverting the process is also possible by being cautious. This procedure is dependent only on the unique circumstances (a fun event versus an arbitrary meeting among total outsiders in a city), the character ("contemplative individual versus outgoing personality") and your way of life.

Anticipating positive body language is best done by removing all obstacles.

Do you remember how your relative or friend welcomed you home after a long journey? They may have spread their arms out and reached for you with their palms as though they were reaching for something far off. This is a truly positive and open-hearted gesture that warms the soul.

All things considered, you cannot use this positioning under any circumstances with everyone. Your supervisor might be suspicious if you see this position. They may also speculate that your brain has taken some time off. However, comparative signals can help you to use positive body language and remain open to fair and positive.

Your willingness to leave your hands open shows you are genuine and have nothing to hide. It is an indication that you can be trusted. You can also look for other signs to help you recognize earnestness or collaboration.

* Keep your body straight to attain certainty and vital

* Make sure you keep great eye contact. It shows tha

* Don't bow to the other person, but keep your head

* Do not hold objects or place them on your body.

* Smile.

It is simple. To like someone, you have to be close to them. The closer you become to someone, the more curious you will be. In order to express non-verbally, it is best to move forward with gestures or grinning.

Does that imply that you should incline and gesture constantly?

No. This is a mistake.

1. If you extend your incline too far, you can make it difficult for another person. This is the reason we tend to incline forward to threaten our enemy. It is also the reason we tend not to go as far as we should.

2. If you constantly gesture, grin, and incline with others, you will undoubtedly seem anxious to ask if it's okay. In this manner, your status is lowered.

As an analogy, think of inclining as driving. The more gas you put on, the more drawn in, and excited you are. However, the less gas you use, the casualter and more distant you feel. It doesn't matter if you are slipping to the limit. You can also interchange your "speed" to adapt to the circumstances.

Additionally, just as with driving, the course and direction of an incline have essentials. We subliminally incline and move toward the spots or things that we need.

BODY LANGUAGE COMMUNICATION

The body can also be used to identify feelings. A closer look at the body has revealed that stances are more accurate when contrasted with a different or unbiased feeling. An example of this is a man feeling angry. His stance would suggest he prefers strength to the other. Contrast this with the feeling of being dreadful. A man would feel weak, docile, their stance would reflect their avoidance tendencies, the opposite of a furious individual.

Emotions can also be expressed by a person's sitting or standing position. Sitting down with their head up and gesturing along the dialogue, a man indicates they are open and free to the ideas. A man who is not able to cross his legs or kick their foot marginally while sitting in a chair suggests they are interested and disengaged from the conversation.

If a man stands and holds his arms up, with his feet pointed toward the speaker, it could be argued that they are conscious of the conversation and are open to having a good exchange. A distinction in this stance could be a significant thing, however. Bali regards discourteousness in those who keep their arms open.

It is possible to also effectively alter testosterone and cortisol levels by nonverbal poses. These effects have clear implications for the investigation and analysis of human conduct.

CONFIDENT BODY LANGUAGE

How does it happen that some people seem to be certain while others seem uncertain? If you can make others believe that you are certain, they might trust you more. In the event that they think you are uncertain, how can they accept your statements as valid?

Still

The signs of restlessness are obvious. Their bodies are always moving, sometimes in jerky development that doubles their pressure.

Standing

A restless individual will usually feel 'cheerful feet' when they stand. Someone is more open to staying put, and not moving.

With your feet spaced at a hip-width apart, adjust your weight in a fair way. If your weight is on one side, you have the right to move. You are now immovable, and you can show that you want to stay.

Sitting

Put your head down and relax while sitting. For unwinding, you might place your hands behind your head or on your lap. Or you might steeple your arms when making evaluative judgments.

The lower body should be still. Keep your feet flat on ground, or cross your legs for support. You may feel uneasy if your legs move in an unusual way.

Head

It is simple to show certainty by keeping your head still. Individuals who are constantly on edge seek out dangers. For those who are on edge, it is important to agree on a single point. This will help you stay focused.

Keep your head up and keep your button at the level of your crown. To protect their necks, people tend to place the button on the edge.

Arms

We often move our arms when speaking or attach them when in doubt. Even though you can make minor changes, they can be left to their own devices, such as resting on your laps or hanging by you. You may find a certain standard position where your hands are held behind or in front of the back. This is what we call the "run of the mill" of sovereignty and presidents. Being nervous about your hands can be a sign that you are anxious so it is important to be cautious.

Nervousness can manifest as wriggling. Individuals can hold their hands still, without needing to move them or shroud them. Demonstrating your hands is a great way to build certainty. It shows that you're not skittish and have no weapons. It's smart to keep your fingers out of pockets. However, thumbs in pockets can indicate an easygoing certainty.

Chapter 11: 43 Tips For Body Language

According to research 93% of people's impressions are based off their body language and 7% on what they hear.

Extraordinary elite people naturally attract other people. The power of their body language keeps others interested. Elite people know that body language is more valuable than words. In fact, other people will often make unconsciously a ton of quick assumptions about you just a few seconds after meeting.

It is because elite people have a knack for building attraction quickly. They are well aware of the fact that body language and attractiveness is not about maintaining straight or steady eye contact.

"It is all about connecting people within a few moments of meeting them."

Your body language is the best way to make connections with people if you want be an elite person. If there isn't a connection, then there isn't attraction.

You want to be a leader in your field by using your body language. Below are 43 body language tips I've put together that will help to draw people in and have a hypnotic influence on them.

1. Get your Head Nocked

While talking to others, you should keep your head down and nod your head. It helps others relax and shows empathy. People want to feel 'IMPORTANT. If you smile and nod your head, you make people feel important. This is the fastest and most effective way to communicate with others, even without speaking a word.

You can also lightly 'Rub you Chin' as you listen. This bright gesture signals that the listener is fully focused on your words.

2. An Authoritative Gaze

What is the secret behind Elite Leaders' success? Why do Elite Leaders always appear so dominant? Well, it is because they use Business/Authoritative Gaze. The Authoritative gaze will allow you to be 'AUTHORITATIVE & IMPORTANT'.

What is Authoritative gaz?

The leader is usually the one whose eye level is the highest. "Keep your vision line in the region from the eyes to the mid forehead. To be in the Authority's clear view, leaders and elite people use this authoritative gaze. They are therefore always treated with respect and special attention.

Successful leaders and entrepreneurs in groups must maintain this authoritative gaze to prove their 'Elite status'.

3. Your Hair Should Be Straightened by Running Your Fingers Through It

When they aren't sure what to say, people run their fingers across their hair. Anyone who is skilled in body-language can see that the person lacks confidence. He also doesn't know the right words or what to say next. Don't run your fingers through the hairs of people, especially at business meetings and social events.

The act of playing with your hair is quite different. It is considered a sign to flirt and attract in dating.

4. I'm astonished

You can feel down by putting your hands behind the back and pointing your elbows out. This gesture can be clearly seen on television and during matches.

5. Know-It-All

If someone touches their fingertips during a conversation, it is a sign that they are confident about what they are discussing.

In talk shows, you can often see celebrities using this gesture. This gesture is used often by business owners during meetings to help them discuss difficult matters.

6. Blue is my color

If you are walking with your hands in the pockets, it can make you appear depressed. If someone is feeling sad, sad, or depressed about something, he will usually do this.

7. Stroking your chin – "I'm not judging you."

While talking, you may notice people stroking chins with their fingers. It is an indication that the person is trying to judge the other person or hear what they have said. It can also be a sign that a person wants to make a decision about something.

8. Point of Aggression

Pointing your fingers at someone you're talking to is a sign of aggression. Do not do this to your family or friends. This will show your weakness and put you in an unfavorable frame.

9. Tone of Your Voice

This is a useful way to judge others. If you are considered equal by someone, your tone will be similar to theirs. It is possible for someone to speak louder than usual and try to dominate you.

10. Mirroring Actions

It is a common gesture. You may notice that someone is mimicking your actions. This can be an indication that they are trying impress you and build rapport. If you feel that someone mirrors your actions, then it is possible to confirm it by changing your body postures and gestures.

11. I'm thinking about You

It is possible that people looking up from the left side are thinking about you, the past, or trying remember something.

12. Pulling the Ear- "What to do?"

If someone pulls his ear it is most likely that he has doubts or is uncertain about something.

13. There's Something Fishy

Someone who touches or lightly rubs their nose in a strange way could be having doubts. It is possible that he is lying to the you. Be careful next time.

14. I'm Not Inquired

If you see someone playing with his phone, pen or paper while you are speaking to him, that means he may not be interested in your words or is trying avoid you. It is also a sign that you are careless and not interested in what you have to say. Because it can make you look unfriendly.

15. Make Me Smile

Do you ever notice that when you smile at someone, they smile back at you? Psychology says it's because our subconsciously mimic the things we see. People tend to smile when they see someone smiling at them. This is a useful and powerful gesture that can encourage others to look at you in positive ways.

16. I'm Frustrated

If you see someone rubbing his hair with their fingers, you can be sure that he is upset about something. This gesture should be avoided. It can be a sign you are frustrated, and it can make your positive aura less.

17. It's amazing!

In disbelief, someone may look down or turn away. If you notice this gesture during conversation, you will know where to push your point more clearly and strongly.

18. Winning The Audience

When they anticipate something, people will often begin to rub their palms (or both) when they are excited. If you notice people doing this gesture, it means that they are interested and excited about what you are going to share with them.

19. Keep your drink intake low

Do not place your drink in front or behind your body when sharing a glass of wine with someone. Instead, hold the drink beside your leg. Keep it close to your body. This will reduce the psychological distance you have with the person you are in contact. Other people don't feel as connected to you on an emotional level.

20. I Feel Fine with You

You can use hand gestures that keep you palms up, such as the "Hands Up" gesture. This gesture is a sign of friendliness and openness. People trust you and feel good around them.

21. It's Your Turn to Make It Interesting

If someone looks in your direction during a conversation, it is an indication that you have successfully triggered their interest in you.

22. I Can Understand What You're Saying

Pay attention to the strongest points when listening to others. This silent gesture demonstrates that you are actively listening to what others are saying and shows that they understand. You use this gesture if you disagree with others but think some points are reasonable.

23. I'm The Champion

The sign of superiority is when your hands are clasped behind the head and your legs cross. This position is common for those who are working on a challenging task or have finished an assignment first.

24. Avoid Multitasking

Avoid multitasking. It's bad. It's a sign of a complex personality. Instead, you should focus on your target and handle each task as a separate entity. It will save you time and keep positive energy around.

25. Lion's Eye

When talking to someone, focus your eyes. It can be difficult to keep your eyes focused while talking with someone.

26. Don't stand too close

If you stand too close to someone, they will feel uncomfortable. Maintain a distance of at least four feet from someone. You can go further, but only with your closest friends and/or your lover.

27. Won't Let You Get Over Me

You can show aggression and dominance by keeping your hands down. You must choose carefully when to keep the palms down and when they should be raised.

28. Do not leave me alone

Your lack interest in the world is evident by not looking up and keeping your head lower than usual. This can be perceived as arrogance, by some people. Keep your head straight while maintaining eye contact with those around you.

29. Toffee eyes

High blinking rates are a sign that you are nervous. If you are anxious about something, your eye blinking rate will increase. When you start feeling nervous, be calm and slow down the rate of your eye blinks. You are likely to blink rapidly with nervousness if you have toffee or swollen eyes.

30. I'm about ready to commit suicide

Sitting on the edge your chair can be a sign that you are feeling uneasy. It can also make people around you uncomfortable.

31. I Want to Quit this Conversation

You shouldn't change your body weight more often than you have to when having a conversation. This can lead to people thinking you want the conversation to end.

32. You are very special to me

Smile with a tilted or tilted face is one way to show genuine likeness. If you see someone smiling with a tilted forehead while they talk to you it's a sign they like and are happy to chat with you.

33. Touch Me

Be aware of your partner's actions when you're out with them. If they touch their necks or thighs while looking at them, it's likely that they want to start a sexual relationship.

34. Quit Ninja Style

You can take small steps while you walk. It will reduce your personality. It shows you aren't confident. Confident people are not afraid to take large steps. They instead take huge steps to be confident and authoritative.

35. Warm Palms

For a great first impression, a firm handshake can be very helpful. Handshakes that are not warm can be interpreted as enthusiasm. A handshake with cold hands will often leave a bad impression. It is important that you keep your palms warm during social events.

36. I'm on Guard

You can't have socializing if you keep your arms crossed in front. It emits negative energies. It makes you seem reserved.

37. Proper grooming

You can communicate confidence with your body if you have it well groomed. You'll be confident to speak and walk with confidence if your body is well groomed.

38. Make Your Tone Stand Out

Elite people never seem out of their place. They are able to adapt to any situation by changing their clothes. They adjust their clothes according to the occasion. That's why they seem so charismatic.

39. Slow down!

Do not move too fast. You will look nervous. Be in control of yourself. Slow down your body movements to make it stand out. Slow body movements demonstrate your strength.

40. Learn from Heroes

It's not enough to simply learn and perfect gestures; you have to be able to use them in real life. Take a look at the body language used by your heroes. To act like a president, you can watch speeches and videos featuring your favorite president. To look like a Vampire, you can watch movies about them and observe their body language.

This helps you decide how to present yourself to others.

41. Use their Names

Dale Carnegie, a famous author once said, "The sweetest sounds to a person's ear is their names." Talk to people using their names. While it doesn't affect your body language, it can help you to improve your body language and add charm.

42. The Magic Touch

While it is difficult to master, this skill can yield powerful results. The areas that need to be touched are the upper arm and shoulders as well as hands. Your fingertips should be used to provide precise touch to these areas, even if you are talking to others. Your touch should be gentle and brief. This helps you build familiarity so others feel close to your touch.

43. Directions indicate attraction

"The body points where the mind wants." Pay attention to people's knees and feet. Because we tend not to look at people we like, we point our feet and knees towards them.

Chapter 12: The Powerful Energy Of The Alpha Male

Alpha males have been around ever since the dawn of humankind. Alpha males win all the girls, success, and power. But how are they able to do this?

Alpha males are able to be present in a way that other males cannot. They have the energy and charisma of the alpha male which makes them stand out from the rest.

They are confident, not just confident. They can move easily through life, without needing any tips or tricks. They are an alpha man.

They don't pretend they are one.

It's what you want, right? You want an alpha male who is genuinely a leader and gets all the perks that alpha men enjoy.

Let's examine how alpha male energie can help you get there!

Why do I need Alpha Male Energy

All women crave the Alpha male energy. It is man in his natural state.

Unfortunately, the majority of men today lack any sort of alpha male energy. This can be attributed to the way society has changed over time.

Alphas no longer existed when humans moved from small "packs", many thousands of years ago. Alpha males weren't needed to guard the pack. And men didn't need to become strong and powerful to survive and pass along their genes.

It was helpful, but it wasn't necessary.

Many men today are conditioned to suppress their natural alpha instincts. A society of men is growing up that suppresses the natural, dominant masculinity and acts like beta males. It is easy to be subservient and avoid the idea that they can use their naturally masculine powers.

Of course, we don't need alpha males but women still want them!

Unfortunately, there are not many alpha males available in today's society. This means that women compete for their attention. Many men settle for the best male beta they can find, rather than waiting until a woman has given up on finding their alpha man. If you're lucky enough to wait long enough you might be able get married to the woman you love, but chances are that you'll end up with someone second-best.

It's easier to attract the woman you want by learning how to project your natural alpha power, than to settle for the one woman who will be happy for you.

What is Alpha Male Energy and How Does It Work?

Alpha male energy can simply be described as a man at his natural state, feeling relaxed in any situation.

This is the same kind of energy as you find in fictional alphas like James Bond and real alphas like George Clooney. Calm, relaxed and powerful.

We've focused on the reaction that women have to the alpha male energy, and the display of this energy. It is more that what you display, and more than the effect it has on other people.

It is something you feel within, a feeling that you have the power to be a man, and a feeling that you can trust wherever you go. Although we tend to focus on the energy being displayed, it's important to realize that it doesn't only have to be shown, but felt.

How to display Alpha Male Energy

Alpha male energy can be displayed by understanding its characteristics and imitating them.

You might be asking why I feel it's so important to "feel it", but then tell you to learn how "show it". This is how we naturally learn.

The first thing children do when they are young is look at their parents and copy what they do. When we are young, we listen to what our parents say and try to emulate them.

This is how we learn best: copying others, even though we don't always know the right way.

When babies are in between the stages of speaking in full sentences and in odd words, they will imitate sentences by repeating non-words in place of the words they understand. They do this because, although they understand from their parents that words are meant for use in sentences, they don't know enough to actually be able to speak in sentences.

It is best to learn something naturally. Spending time with people who speak the language can help you learn it fluently.

The same applies to learning traits like these. You can copy the behavior of an alpha man who fully exhibits it. At first, pretending will work, but as you get more experience, it will become more real and you will begin to display it.

Quick recap

Because of their energy, Alpha males can be irresistible for women. Women crave the calm, powerful, masculine energy that they can feel, regardless of whether it is conscious or not.

Many men today don't understand male energy. As society has developed, it doesn't require an alpha male strong enough to protect the "pack". This has led to a lack in alpha males in society. These are the men that women want and compete for.

Learning how to show alpha male energy will make you stand out from the rest and allow you to choose the women you want.

To display alpha male energies, it is best to allow yourself to feel it and not try to do so. It is best to mimic someone who already displays these characteristics until you can naturally display them.

The Incredible Power of Body Language

How great is your first impression?

You can be judged by people in as little as 30 seconds. The judgments will last for a lifetime. Except if you are a male model, your first impression is largely formed by how you act and how confident you feel.

Your body language can not only influence their first impression of you but also affect how they feel about you when you speak to them. While this may seem unbelievable, it is possible to make a difference with the right body language.

Why is Body Language so Powerful?

One of the greatest influences on your body language lies in the way your subconscious processes it. Contrary to words, which are mostly processed by your conscious brain, body language rarely gets processed consciously.

This can be both in terms your body language or the processing that someone else's body language is.

It is possible to get the feeling of being welcomed by someone who smiles at you. However this will not be something you decide to do. You will also feel happier if you smile, according to research.

This means you can use your body language to communicate effectively with others. It is easy to do this in a short time by learning body language.

How can I harness my body's power?

The power of body language can be used in two steps. The first step in using the power of bodylanguage on yourself to make a powerful improvement in your state, and the second is to better understand how bodylanguage can be used to communicate with others.

This is the easiest step and will only require a few changes in your daily routine.

In just 2 minutes, you can transform your body language and self-esteem

Research shows that body language has the ability to increase your confidence in just 2 minutes. By adopting a "high-power pose", you can quickly eliminate stress and worry, and replace them by power and confidence.

It also showed that the opposite effect could occur. If your focus is on slouching in a "low-power" pose, it will increase your stress levels and worry. In turn, your confidence and power will be lost.

High power poses are those that you can do confidently and with open arms. One example of this is to sit straight ahead with your arms out and your legs spread apart. Or, you could sit with your hands behind your back and look forward while your legs rest on a chair or a table. Or, you can stand with your knees bent and your hands behind your head, with your legs extended to the sides.

These power poses increase your testosterone which in turn increases your dominance and confidence. These two characteristics are known as alpha male. Just 2 minutes of power poses resulted in an increase of testosterone of 8% and a decrease of cortisol of 25%, which can cause stress to rise by 25%.

The opposite was true for those with low-power poses. They had an increase of 15% cortisol, and a decrease by 10% testosterone.

The lowest power pose is closed arms with legs crossed, arms folded and legs together looking down at floor.

Now, ask yourself this question: Where do you usually stand? Do you always assume the high-power pose? Or do you choose to unconsciously adopt the low power position?

You can see the effects of testosterone on you in just two minutes. But how big could a lifetime be?

It is important to start slowly by taking time to hold these powerful poses for just a few minutes each day. A mere 2 minute a day can give you the boost that you need to feel more powerful, confident, and empowered. The power poses can be used to give you a boost prior to an important event (e.g. a date, going out with friends or simply speaking to women). You can also do power poses throughout the day to boost your energy for the day.

You should aim to strengthen your unconscious body language over time so that you can feel confident. It's impossible to change your body language overnight. Instead, the best thing to do is to practice adjusting your body language to be more powerful.

This was done by standing tall and looking straight ahead whenever I walked past a door.

It was almost as though the door had a pull at my head that straightened my body and placed me in the perfect position. This is a good idea because you're likely to pass through a door many times each day. You can adjust your stance every time by simply standing taller.

Although it may take some time to get used to it at first, it will become more natural over time. Your new, powerful stance will gradually become the way you stand. Imagine how much more confident you'll be after one month of naturally walking with high-power stance. The positive impact it will have on your daily life will be immense.

Therefore, you must get started immediately!

Communicate with Others by Using the Power of Body Language

If you have spent your entire life believing that 55% is communicated through your body, you will have used your body to communicate more effectively with others.

The chances are you didn't get the best from your work because of how your body language was used.

Congruence, which simply means that your body language is the same as your words, is one of many great ways body language can improve your communication. Imagine your boss sitting on his stomach, biting down on his nails, and saying, "I am completely in control of the office. I'm going to get back to my work." Would you believe him. Or did you just feel something wasn't right? Or, imagine if he stood in front of you and pointed out from the office while he said it. I'm sure that you'd believe him.

The most important thing Dr. discovered in his research was how different communication methods affected the likeability and dislikeability of a person. The study found that people were more likeable when their words and actions were consistent. This is why, when you approach a woman and make a casual, direct comment, they are more likely than others to accept it. Your body language should be confident, with a smile and a willingness to listen. Your body language and expressions are indicative of confidence.

This is why men may walk up to women with the most casual of conversation lines and then leave the club together. Others will be laughed out of their clubs if they try the same thing.

Your outward image of self-assurance and confidence will be displayed by your strong, alpha masculine body language. Also, you must back up everything you say verbally and non-verbally. A friendly comment or a joke needs to be backed by a smile. A genuine compliment should be accompanied by eye contact and smile. It will be difficult for the other person to see the connection and feel the distrust or dislike.

As you read the book, you'll learn how to use body language. For now, however, it is important to remember that your verbal communication should be supported by non-verbal communication.

Chapter 13: What Our Body Does

Your body language is how we communicate with our outside world. And even though the majority of us don't get it, we are speaking the truth! The core of who you are, as an individual, is affected tremendously by body language. It has a profound impact on our posture and physiological health. However, it can also affect our psychological outlook, how we see the world, and how others perceive us.

What our body does

Our body language allows us to express our thoughts, feelings and musings. We communicate with purposeful actions like applauding or shrugging our shoulders, as well as inadvertently by twisting in our faces or guiding the feet in another direction towards the person we're talking to. Before spoken language existed, body language was our primary method of communication. Our

157

primary method of communicating with other people is via our bodies.

How can it affect our mind?

While our body language is how the outside world interacts with us, it is also how we communicate with ourselves. How would your body language affect how you treat yourself? Are you content to walk straight and confident? It's true that you are grateful for every opportunity your body offers you.

Most likely, not. We regularly underestimate our bodies and often choose to decry them. The body language we use can have a significant impact on our posture and physical body. However, it can also change our mood. A positive attitude can make it easier to cope with stress and lower your misery.

Installed comprehension, which is a rapidly growing field of psychology, asserts that our body's relationship with our surroundings does not only impact us. However, the way we think is shaped by our individual thoughts.

Four Different Ways You Can Change Your Body Language

Below are four methods to alter your body language.

The Glare is on the Other Side!

Smiley faces and laughter are infectious. A comprehensive report on smiling showed that smiling can bring out positive emotions by drawing in the mouth and moving the skin around the eyes. Grin and smile often! It doesn't matter if you're having a bad day or not, smile regardless! It could help you to turn around your day!

Collapsing Your Arms

The resistance system of the heart and lungs can be found at the intersection between the arms. When we feel anxious, shaken, or otherwise disturbed, we often do it. People feel cut off or detached when they experience the physical obstruction.

Crossing the arms is considered an antagonistic body position. Some research has shown that crossing one's arms can cause people to become more productive when they feel like stopping.

Do you think you might need an extra boost in your mental health? Then you can try home-made cures such as Hyperiforce. It contains extracts of the flower hypericum which are often used to treat nervousness and low mood.

Force Presenting

Amy Cuddy is an important specialist in the realm of body language. Before she could send them to a top-weight talk, she made sure they remained in both high force stances as well as low force models for two minute. She measured levels of the stress hormone cortisol as well as the dominant hormone testosterone. The results showed that those in high-force presence had greater testosterone degrees and lower cortisol levels compared to those in less force.

Quit Slumping

Slumping may not be obvious at first glance, but it can also affect your spine. It can also alter your mind. It can even cause an abnormal spine arrangement and agony. It can also make you feel sluggish, depressed and disconnected from others. Sitting down and standing straighter can ease the pain, as well as improve your quality of life.

Changes in your posture can be hard on your body, especially if your body is used to sitting down for prolonged periods. The neck, back, and muscles may hurt. It's normal, but don't worry, it will pass. Atrogel can be used to relieve discomfort. It contains new arnica bloom concentrates.

Enhance your posture to improve the quality of your temperament

It's unlikely that body language is the first sport you would think of when feeling down. Our body language can show us what our true feelings are. Just as our moods are affected by how we look, our body language can also influence our posture.

You can adjust your mindset by changing your posture in these simple steps:

* Smile when it is a bad day

* Relax your arms when you feel anxious.

* Moving forward with your hands, rather than moving ahead, will cause the shoulders and arms to move in a more relaxed manner.

* Power must be present before it is possible to instigate situations such as potential employee meetups.

Signs in your body language that someone is hiding something from you

Untrustworthiness. It's a problem that can be found in many relationships. Once in awhile, it's a good idea to keep secret information from your accomplice during a relationship. Your accomplice does not need to know everything about your lives. This is simply insolent. It is an indication that you don't care enough about your accomplice to understand that they are worthy of reality. It is saying that you don't trust your accomplice enough to discern what's true. This is terrible for any relationship. You need to tell your accomplice everything, especially concerning the important aspects of your relationship.

It is true that many people are very childish. It's not always easy to take in the reality. Sometimes, the truth can make us feel like we are carrying a heavy burden. We will often lie just for the sake of our sanity. You may be guilty of telling such lies. He could be keeping your man from telling you about things he should have told you.

Furthermore, it can be hazardous for a partnership. Without the best possible reality, you can't expect your link to work. To ensure you don't get swindled or bushwhacked, it is essential that you fully understand what is happening.

Men aren't the best communicators. You might already be aware of this. It doesn't matter what, he communicates with you through his body language. He may reveal many things to you about himself through his intuitive abilities, even though you don't see it. All you have to do is to openly and willingly give your support to spot any signs. You have to be consistent in your control of the relationship.

Understanding and Receiving Nonverbal Signs

Lauren murmured. Gus, Lauren's chief, sent her an email explaining that the item proposition she had been considering was not being closed. It didn't bode well. Seven days previously, she'd been to a gathering along with Gus, where he had appeared extremely positive about everything. He continued looking out the window, even though he didn't see. However, she recently put that down as him being occupied. Additionally, he said that "the task most likely will stretch the go beyond."

Lauren could have understood, if she had stumbled upon some body language lessons, that Gus was trying tell her that he didn't "sell" her thinking. He didn't use words.

The Most Effective Way to Read Negative Body Text

Monitor negative body language and emotions in others can help you identify hidden issues or distress. This area will also highlight negative nonverbal signals that you should pay particular attention to.

Troublesome Conversations, Defensiveness

Talking about difficult or stressful topics is an unpleasant truth. Maybe you had to manage a client who was annoying or to have a conversation with them about their horrible showing. Maybe you've even managed to arrange a significant agreement.

In a perfect universe, such circumstances would lead to peace and calm. Be that as it might, their lives are often filled with feelings of fear, anxiety, stress and preventiveness. They may be able to be hidden, and these feelings are often visible in our body language. A person who is engaging in at least one or more of these behaviors will most likely be withdrawing, uninvolved, and/or miserable.

* Arms fell before the body.

* Outwardly, insignificant or tense

* The body took some distance from you.

* Eyes depressed, keeping in touch.

* Avoiding unengaged Audiences

If you need to give an introduction, or collaborate in a group setting, the people around you must be 100 percent committed. Here are some obvious signs that someone might not be paying attention to what you are stating.

* Sitting, head down and droopy.

* Looking at something completely different or into space.

* Squirming and picking at clothing, or tinkering around with pens, telephones, and pens.

* She was composing and doodling.

Step by step instructions to project positive body language

Positive body language adds solidarity to verbal messages and thoughts. To increase fearlessness as well as receptiveness, there are some basic postures you can adopt.

Establishing a Trustful First Connection

These tips will assist you in adapting your body language so that you can establish an extraordinary first relationship.

* Pose with an open attitude. Be loose; however, don't slump! Your hands should be at your sides. Refrain from putting your hands on the hips. It will make you seem larger and more authoritative, which can lead to animosity or a desire to rule.

* Utilize a firm handshake. Be calm and not too energetic. It doesn't have the potential to become unbalanced for you or more regrettable, even excruciatingly painful for your partner. You'll probably appear to be rude or forceful in the event it does.

* Keep in touch. Maintain eye contact for a few moments with the other person, one after the next. It will let her know that you are correct and in control. Do not turn it into an eye-rolling match.

* Try to avoid touching your face. The common sense is that those who approach their face while asking questions are untrustworthy. It is possible to make mistakes with your hair and contact your nose while trying to trust others.

Chapter 14: The 6 Types Basic Emotions, And Their Effects On Human Behavior

There are many types of emotions that influence our behavior and interactions with others. It can feel like these emotions are controlling us at times. All of our actions and perceptions are influenced by the emotions that we experience at any given time.

Psychologists have tried to determine the types of emotions people experience. A variety of theories have been developed to explain and categorize emotions.

Paul Eckman, psychologist in the 1970s, identified six basic emotions which he believed were universally experienced across all cultures. He identified the emotions as happiness, sadness, fear of, disgust, terror, surprise, and anger. He added to his list of basic emotions by including pride, shame embarrassment, excitement, and anger.

Combining Emotions. Robert Plutchik, psychologist, proposed a "wheel for emotions" which works in the same way as the color wheel. Emotions can be combined in order to create different emotions, just as colors can be mixed together to create other shades. According to this theory, basic emotions work as building blocks. The blending of more complex and sometimes mixed emotions is called "building blocks". It is possible to combine basic emotions, such as joy and trust, to create love.

A 2017 study found that there are far more basic emotions to be human than was previously believed. The study, published in Proceedings of National Academy of Sciences (PNA), identified 27 different types of emotion. Researchers discovered that the emotions experienced by people are not always distinct.

Let's take an in-depth look at some basic emotions to see their effect on human behavior.

Happiness

Happiness, out of all the possible emotions, is the one people most desire. Happiness is often defined by a happy state of mind that is marked by joy, contentment, gratification and satisfaction. In a variety of fields, research on happiness has increased dramatically since 1960s. Positive psychology is one example.

This type of emotion may be expressed by:

* Face expressions like smiling

* Body language, such as a relaxed posture

* A cheerful, positive tone of voice

Happiness is an emotion that can be described as the core of human nature. But, cultural influences heavily influence our beliefs about what will make us happy. Pop culture influences, for instance, emphasize the importance of having a good job or buying a house to bring you happiness. Sometimes, the realities of what contributes to happiness can be more complex and highly personalized.

It has been a long-held belief that happiness and well-being are connected. However, research has shown that happiness may play a role both in mental and physical health. Happiness has been associated with a range of outcomes, including higher longevity and greater marital satisfaction.

Unhappiness has been linked in a variety of negative health outcomes. Anxiety, stress and depression have all been associated with decreased immunity, increased inflammation, and a shorter life expectancy.

Sadness

Sadness is another emotion that can be defined as a temporary emotional state. It's characterized by sadness, anger, grief, hopelessness or disinterest and can often be described as a feeling of sadness.

All people experience sadness from time to another, as do other emotions. In extreme cases, sadness can become debilitating.

There are many ways that sadness can be expressed, including:

* Dampened mood

* Quietness

* Lethargy

* Withdrawal of others

* Crying

The severity and type, as well as the cause, of sadness can vary. Also, how people deal with them can differ.

Sadness can cause people to resort to self-medicating, avoidance, and negative thinking in order to cope. These behaviors can actually worsen the sadness and extend the feeling.

Fear

Fear can be a powerful emotion and play an important part in survival. Fear can be experienced when you face danger or fear. This is called the "fight or flight" response. Your muscles will become tighter, your heartbeat and respiration will increase, and you'll feel more alert. These responses can prepare your body for either running from the danger or fighting back. This allows you to respond quickly to threats in your environment.

Expressions that express this kind of emotion include:

* Facial expressions include enlarging the eyes and pulling the chin down

* Attempts of hiding or fleeing the threat

* Physiological reactions (e.g. rapid breathing, heartbeat)

Everyone experiences fear differently. Different people might be more fearful than others, and some situations or objects could trigger this emotion more.

Fear is an emotional response to an immediate threat. It is possible to have a similar reaction when faced with anticipated dangers or our thoughts about potential dangers. This is what we call anxiety. Social anxiety, for instance, is the anticipation of fear in social situations.

However, there are some people who seek out fear-provoking situations. Although extreme sports and other thrilling activities can be scary, some people find that they thrive in these situations and even enjoy them.

Exposure to a fear object or situation repeatedly can lead to familiarity, which can reduce anxiety and fear. This is what exposure therapy is all about. People are slowly exposed to things that frighten their in a safe and controlled way. Gradually, fear begins to lessen.

Disgust

Eckman described disgust as one of six basic emotions. Disgust can be expressed in a variety of ways.

* Turning your back on the object in disgust

* Physical reactions (e.g. vomiting or retching).

* Facial expressions: e.g., wrinkling the nose, curling the upper lips.

The sensation of revulsion may be caused by a variety of things, such as an unpleasant smell, taste or sight. Researchers believe that this emotion was developed in response to food that could be dangerous or even fatal. For example, disgust occurs when people taste or smell bad foods.

Infection, blood, rot and death can all trigger disgust responses. This may be the body's way to avoid possible transmittable diseases. If they witness others engaging in actions they find disgusting, immoral, and evil, it can lead to moral disgust.

Anger

Anger can be a strong emotion. It is characterised by hostility to others, agitation and frustration. Like fear, anger may play a part of your body's fight/flight response. If you feel angry about a threat, it is possible to be more inclined to defend yourself and fend off the danger.

Anger often manifests itself through:

* Facial expressions (e.g. frowning, glaring)

* Body language: This could include taking a firm someone.

* Tone such as gruff or yelling

* Physiological responses, such as sweating and turni

* Aggressive behaviors like hitting, kicking or throwir

While anger is usually viewed negatively, it can sometimes turn out to be a good thing. It can be helpful in clarifying your needs in a relationship and can motivate you and drive you to find solutions.

But anger can cause problems if it is uncontrolled or expressed in unhealthy, dangerous, and harmful ways to others. Uncontrolled anger can quickly lead to aggression and violence.

This emotion can have both psychological and physical consequences. Unchecked anger can make decisions difficult and have a negative effect on your health.

Anger has been linked with heart disease and diabetes. Anger can also be linked to unhealthy behaviors such as aggressive driving and alcohol consumption.

Surprise

Eckman first described surprise as another of the six basic emotions of humans. Surprise is often very brief and is characterized in a physiological startle response after something unexpected.

This type of emotion could be positive, neutral, or negative. For example, an unpleasant surprise might be someone leaping from behind a branch and scaring you on your way to your car at nights. You might find your best friends gathering at home to celebrate your birthday.

Surprising is often characterized as:

* Facial expressions: Lifting the eyebrows, widening your eyes, or opening your mouth.

* Physical responses like jumping back

* Verbal reactions like screaming, shouting, or gasping

Another type of emotion that can cause the fight or flee response is surprise. When people are surprised, they may feel an adrenaline rush that prepares them to fight or flee.

The power of surprise can have a significant impact on our behavior. Research has shown people tend to be more aware of surprising events. This is why unusual and unexpected news events tend to stick out in people's minds more than others. Research also suggests that people are more likely than others to listen to unexpected arguments and to absorb surprising information more easily.

There are other types of emotions

Eckman only describes six fundamental emotions. They are just a fraction of the many types of emotions people can experience. Eckman believes that these core emotions are universal in cultures around the globe. But, there are many theories and new research that continue to explore the many types and classifications for emotions.

Eckman later added more emotions to his initial six, but said that none of these could be encoded using facial expressions. He identified some of these emotions later:

There are other theories of emotion:

Not all psychology theorists agree how to classify emotions. Eckman's theory remains the most popular, but there are many other theories that offer their own views on the essence of human emotion.

Research suggests that there may be only two or three basic emotions. Others suggested that emotions can be arranged in a hierarchy. Secondary emotions, such as sadness, joy, surprise and anger, can be then broken down into their primary emotions. The secondary emotions that make up love, such as affection or longing, are, for instance, joy, surprise, anger, sadness, and love.

These secondary emotions can then be broken down further into what are known tertiary emotional. Tertiary emotions such as compassion, liking, caring, and tenderness are all part of the secondary emotion affection.

A recent study found that there are at minimum 27 distinct emotions. Each of them is interconnected. Researchers created an interactive map that shows the relationships between these emotions after analyzing responses from more than 800 men to over 2000 video clips.

Dacher Keltner is a senior researcher at the Greater Good Science Center and the faculty director. "We discovered that 27 dimensions were needed, not six."

This means that emotions don't exist in isolation. Instead, the study suggests there are gradients in emotion and that these feelings are deeply interrelated.

Alan Cowen (the study's principal author and doctoral candidate in neuroscience at UC Berkeley) suggests that better understanding emotions can play a significant role in helping scientists and psychologists learn more about brain activity and behavior. He hopes that better treatment for mental conditions can be developed by researchers who have a better understanding of these states.

Conclusion

Everyday life is enriched by body language. It would be very difficult to discern the true meaning behind people's actions and words without body language. It is important to take into account many aspects of body communication when trying to figure out what a person means. Be aware that facial expressions as well as eye movement, perspiration and breathing can all be considered body language.

These things are easy to forget or ignore. However, people who pay attention and understand body language actually have an advantage over others who don't. People who are able and willing to pay attention to body language can often be characterized as intelligent people.

A person with a high sense of awareness and heightened senses of surroundings would make a great star witness in a crime. That person would be capable of telling authorities everything about the suspect, from the color of their shoes to the tattoos that may have been on their bodies.

It is vital to learn body language. However, body language can be misleading. It is possible for a person to speak in different ways than their body language, which can sometimes be subconsciously. It is therefore important to focus on context clues, and ensure you get all details from a conversation.